THE BATTLE OF FRANKLIN

THE LOCHLAINN SEABROOK COLLECTION

CONSTITUTIONAL HISTORY
The Articles of Confederation Explained: A Clause-by-Clause Study of America's First Constitution
The Constitution of the Confederate States of America Explained: A Clause-by-Clause Study of
    the South's Magna Carta

VICTORIAN CONFEDERATE LITERATURE
Rise Up and Call Them Blessed: Victorian Tributes to the Confederate Soldier, 1861-1901
The God of War: Nathan Bedford Forrest As He Was Seen By His Contemporaries
The Old Rebel: Robert E. Lee As He Was Seen By His Contemporaries
Victorian Confederate Poetry: The Southern Cause in Verse, 1861-1901

ABRAHAM LINCOLN
Abraham Lincoln: The Southern View - Demythologizing America's Sixteenth President
Lincolnology: The Real Abraham Lincoln Revealed in His Own Words - A Study of Lincoln's
    Suppressed, Misinterpreted, and Forgotten Writings and Speeches
The Great Impersonator! 99 Reasons to Dislike Abraham Lincoln
The Unholy Crusade: Lincoln's Legacy of Destruction in the American South
The Unquotable Abraham Lincoln: The President's Quotes They Don't Want You To Know!

CIVIL WAR BATTLES
Encyclopedia of the Battle of Franklin - A Comprehensive Guide to the Conflict that Changed the
    Civil War
Nathan Bedford Forrest and the Battle of Fort Pillow: Yankee Myth, Confederate Fact
The Battle of Franklin: Recollections of Confederate and Union Soldiers
The Battle of Nashville: Recollections of Confederate and Union Soldiers
The Battle of Spring Hill: Recollections of Confederate and Union Soldiers

PARANORMAL
Carnton Plantation Ghost Stories: True Tales of the Unexplained from Tennessee's Most Haunted
    Civil War House!
UFOs and Aliens: The Complete Guidebook

FAMILY HISTORIES
The Blakeneys: An Etymological, Ethnological, and Genealogical Study - Uncovering the
    Mysterious Origins of the Blakeney Family and Name
The Caudills: An Etymological, Ethnological, and Genealogical Study - Exploring the Name and
    National Origins of a European-American Family
The McGavocks of Carnton Plantation: A Southern History - Celebrating One of Dixie's Most
    Noble Confederate Families and Their Tennessee Home

MIND, BODY, SPIRIT
Autobiography of a Non-Yogi: A Scientist's Journey From Hinduism to Christianity (Dr. Amitava
    Dasgupta, with Lochlainn Seabrook)
Britannia Rules: Goddess-Worship in Ancient Anglo-Celtic Society - An Academic Look at the
    United Kingdom's Matricentric Spiritual Past
Christ Is All and In All: Rediscovering Your Divine Nature and the Kingdom Within
Christmas Before Christianity: How the Birthday of the "Sun" Became the Birthday of the "Son"
Jesus and the Gospel of Q: Christ's Pre-Christian Teachings As Recorded in the New Testament
Jesus and the Law of Attraction: The Bible-Based Guide to Creating Perfect Health, Wealth, and
    Happiness Following Christ's Simple Formula
Seabrook's Bible Dictionary of Traditional and Mystical Christian Doctrines
The Bible and the Law of Attraction: 99 Teachings of Jesus, the Apostles, and the Prophets
The Book of Kelle: An Introduction to Goddess-Worship and the Great Celtic Mother-Goddess
    Kelle, Original Blessed Lady of Ireland
The Goddess Dictionary of Words and Phrases: Introducing a New Core Vocabulary for the
    Women's Spirituality Movement
The Way of Holiness: The Story of Religion and Myth From the Cave Bear Cult to Christianity

WOMEN
Aphrodite's Trade: The Hidden History of Prostitution Unveiled
Princess Diana: Modern Day Moon-Goddess - A Psychoanalytical and Mythological Look at Diana
    Spencer's Life, Marriage, and Death (with Dr. Jane Goldberg)
Women in Gray: A Tribute to the Ladies Who Supported the Southern Confederacy

Five-Star Books & Gifts From the Heart of the American South
SeaRavenPress.com

Warning:
SEA RAVEN PRESS
BOOKS WILL EXPAND
YOUR ★ MIND!

THE BATTLE OF

FRANKLIN

Recollections of Confederate & Union Soldiers

Collected, Edited, & Arranged, with an Introduction by the author,
"The Voice of the Traditional South," Colonel

LOCHLAINN SEABROOK

JEFFERSON DAVIS HISTORICAL GOLD MEDAL WINNER

Diligently Researched and Generously
Illustrated for the Elucidation of the Reader

2018

Sea Raven Press, Nashville, Tennessee, USA

THE BATTLE OF FRANKLIN

Published by
Sea Raven Press, Cassidy Ravensdale, President
PO Box 1484, Spring Hill, Tennessee 37174-1484 USA
SeaRavenPress.com • searavenpress@gmail.com

SEA RAVEN PRESS
SOUTHERN BOOKS, REAL HISTORY!

1ˢᵗ SRP paperback edition, 1ˢᵗ printing, October 2018 • ISBN: 978-1-943737-75-8
1ˢᵗ SRP hardcover edition, 1ˢᵗ printing, October 2018 • ISBN: 978-1-943737-76-5

ISBN: 978-1-943737-75-8 (paperback)
Library of Congress Control Number: 2018960449

The Battle of Franklin: Recollections of Confederate and Union Soldiers, by Lochlainn Seabrook. Includes endnotes, maps, appendices, and bibliographical references.

All persons who approve of the authority and principles of Colonel Lochlainn Seabrook's literary work, and realize its benefits as a means of reeducating the world about the South and the Confederacy, are hereby requested to avidly recommend his books to others and to vigorously cooperate in extending their reach, scope, and influence around the globe.

The views on the American "Civil War" documented in this book are those of the publisher.

PRINTED & MANUFACTURED IN OCCUPIED TENNESSEE, FORMER CONFEDERATE STATES OF AMERICA

SEA RAVEN PRESS

DEDICATION

To my Confederate kindred at Franklin, November 30, 1864. Your names are your monuments.

(Photo Lochlainn Seabrook)

EPIGRAPH

"Next to a great defeat, the saddest thing in the world is a great victory."

THE FIRST DUKE OF WELLINGTON
1769-1852

"Battle of Franklin," chromolithograph, 1891.

CONTENTS

SEA
RAVEN
PRESS

SEA RAVEN PRESS

THE WORLD'S #1 SOUTH-FRIENDLY BOOK PUBLISHER

Restoring Dixie's honor
Defending traditional Southern culture
Preserving authentic Confederate history
One book at a time!

Nashville, Tennessee

SeaRavenPress.com

NOTES TO THE READER

**"NOTHING IN THE PAST IS DEAD TO THE MAN WHO WOULD
LEARN HOW THE PRESENT CAME TO BE WHAT IT IS."**

WILLIAM STUBBS, VICTORIAN ENGLISH HISTORIAN

THE TWO MAIN POLITICAL PARTIES IN 1860

☛ In any study of America's antebellum, bellum, and postbellum periods, it is vitally important to understand that in 1860 the two major political parties—the Democrats and the newly formed Republicans—were the opposite of what they are today. In other words, the Democrats of the mid 19th Century were Conservatives, akin to the Republican Party of today, while the Republicans of the mid 19th Century were Liberals, akin to the Democratic Party of today.[1]

Thus the Confederacy's Democratic president, Jefferson Davis, was a Conservative (with libertarian leanings); the Union's Republican president, Abraham Lincoln, was a Liberal (with socialistic leanings).[2] This is why, in the mid 1800s, the conservative wing of the Democratic Party was known as "the States' Rights Party."[3]

The author's cousin, Confederate Vice President and Democrat Alexander H. Stephens: a Southern Conservative.

Hence, the Democrats of the Civil War period referred to themselves as "conservatives," "confederates," "anti-centralists," or "constitutionalists" (the latter because they favored strict adherence to the original Constitution—which tacitly guaranteed states' rights—as created by the Founding Fathers), while the Republicans called themselves "liberals," "nationalists," "centralists," or "consolidationists" (the latter three because they wanted to nationalize the central government and consolidate political power in Washington, D.C.).[4]

Since this idea is new to most of my readers, let us further demystify it by viewing it from the perspective of the American Revolutionary War. If Davis and his conservative Southern constituents (the Democrats of 1861) had been alive in 1775, they would have sided with George Washington and the American colonists, who sought to secede from the tyrannical government of Great Britain; if Lincoln and his Liberal Northern constituents (the Republicans of 1861) had been alive at that time, they would have sided with King George III and the English monarchy, who sought to maintain the American colonies as possessions of the British Empire. It is due to this very comparison that Southerners often refer to their secession as the Second Declaration of Independence and the "Civil War" as the Second American Revolutionary War.

Without a basic understanding of these facts, the American "Civil War" will forever remain incomprehensible. For a full discussion of this topic see my book, *Abraham Lincoln Was a Liberal, Jefferson Davis Was a Conservative: The Missing Key to Understanding the American Civil War.*

THE TERM "CIVIL WAR"

☛ As I heartily dislike the phrase "Civil War," its use throughout this book (as well as in my other works) is worthy of explanation.

Our entire modern literary system refers to the conflict of 1861 using the Northern term the "Civil War," whether we in the South like it or not. Of course, this is purposeful, for America's book industry, which determines everything from how books are categorized and designed to how they are marketed and sold, is almost solely controlled by Liberals, socialists, globalists, collectivists, and communists, individuals who will do anything to prevent the truth about Lincoln's War from coming out. An important aspect of this wholesale revisionism of American

The American "Civil War" was not a true civil war as Webster defines it: "A conflict between opposing groups of citizens of the *same* country." It was a fight between two individual countries; or to be more specific, two separate and constitutionally formed confederacies: the U.S.A. and the C.S.A.

history is the use of the phrase "Civil War," which Yankee Liberals thrust into the public forum even as big government Left-winger Lincoln was diabolically tricking the Conservative South into firing the first shot at the Battle of Fort Sumter in April 1861.

The progressives' blatant American "Civil War" coverup continues to this day, one of the more overt results which pertains to how books are coded, indexed, and identified.[5] Thus, as all book searches by readers, libraries, and retail outlets are now performed online, and as all bookstores categorize works from or about this period under the heading "Civil War," honest book publishers and authors who deal with this particular topic have little choice but to use this deceptive term. If I were to refuse to use it, as some of my Southern colleagues have suggested, few people would ever find or read my books.

Add to this the fact that scarcely any non-Southerners have ever heard of the names we in the South use for the conflict, such as the "War for Southern Independence"——or my personal preference, "Lincoln's War." It only makes sense then to use the term "Civil War" in most commercial situations, historically inaccurate though it is.

We should also bear in mind that while today educated persons, particularly educated Southerners, all share an abhorrence for the phrase "Civil War," it was not always so. Confederates who lived through and even fought in the conflict regularly used the term throughout the 1860s, and even long after. Among them were Confederate generals such as Nathan Bedford Forrest, Richard Taylor, and Joseph E. Johnston, not to mention the Confederacy's vice president, Alexander H. Stephens.

Confederate General Nathan Bedford Forrest, just one of many Southern officials who referred to the conflict of 1861 as the "Civil War."

In 1895 Confederate General James Longstreet wrote about his military experiences in a work subtitled, *Memoirs of the Civil War in America*, while in 1903 Confederate General John Brown Gordon entitled his autobiography, *Reminiscences of the Civil War*. Even the Confederacy's highest leader, President Jefferson Davis, used the term "Civil War,"[6] and in one case at least, as late as 1881——the year he wrote his brilliant exposition, *The Rise and Fall of the Confederate Government*.[7] Authors writing for *Confederate Veteran* magazine sometimes used the phrase well into the early 1900s,[8] and in 1898, at the Eighth Annual Meeting and Reunion of the United Confederate Veterans (the forerunner of today's Sons of Confederate Veterans), the following resolution was proposed: that from then on the Great War of 1861 was to be designated "the Civil War Between the States."[9]

A WORD ON EARLY AMERICAN MATERIAL

☛ In order to preserve the authentic historicity of the antebellum, bellum, and postbellum periods, I have retained the original spellings, formatting, and punctuation of the early Americans I quote. These include such items as British-English spellings, long-running paragraphs, obsolete words, and various literary devices peculiar to the time. However, I have corrected misspelled names to prevent confusion, and also *where possible*, inaccurate dates and locations (the inevitable result of old faulty memories). Bracketed words within quotes are my additions and clarifications, while italicized words within quotes are (where indicated) my emphasis.

PRESENTISM

☞ As a historian I view *presentism* (judging the past according to present day mores and customs) as the enemy of authentic history. And this is precisely why the Left employs it in its ongoing war against traditional American, conservative, and Christian values. By looking at history through the lens of modern day beliefs—and, just as heinous, fabricating obviously fake history based on emotion, opinion, and political ideology—they are able to distort, revise, and reshape the past into a false narrative that fits their ideological agenda: the liberalization *and* Northernization of America, the enlargement and further centralization of the national government, and total control of American political, economic, and social power, the same agenda that Lincoln championed.[10]

Judging our ancestors by our own standards is dishonest, unfair, unjust, misleading, and unethical.

This book rejects presentism and replaces it with what I call *historicalism*: judging our ancestors based on the values of their own time. To get the most from this work the reader is invited to reject presentism as well. In this way—along with casting aside preconceived notions and the fake history churned out by our left-wing education system—the truth in this work will be most readily ascertained and absorbed; truth that has been rigorously researched and forensically uncovered by myself using the scientific method. As Confederate Colonel Bennett H. Young noted in 1901:

> History is valuable only as it is true. Opinions concerning acts are not history; acts themselves alone are historic.[11]

LEARN MORE

☞ Lincoln's War on the American people and the Constitution can never be fully understood without a thorough knowledge of the South's perspective. As this book is only meant to be a brief introductory guide to these topics, one cannot hope to learn the complete story here. For those who are interested in additional material from Dixie's viewpoint, please see my comprehensive histories listed on pages 2 and 3.

Keep Your Body, Mind, & Spirit Vibrating at Their Highest Level

YOU CAN DO SO BY READING THE BOOKS OF

SEA RAVEN PRESS

There is nothing that will so perfectly keep your body, mind, and spirit in a healthy condition as to think wisely and positively. Hence you should not only read this book, but also the other books that we offer. They will quicken your physical, mental, and spiritual vibrations, enabling you to maintain a position in society as a healthy erudite person.

KEEP YOURSELF WELL-INFORMED!

The well-informed person is always at the head of the procession, while the ignorant, the lazy, and the unthoughtful hang onto the rear. If you are a Spiritual man or woman, do yourself a great favor: read Sea Raven Press books and stay well posted on the Truth. It is almost criminal for one to remain in ignorance while the opportunity to gain knowledge is open to all at a nominal price.

We invite you to visit our Webstore for a wide selection of wholesome, family-friendly, well-researched, educational books for all ages. You will be glad you did!

Five-Star Books & Gifts From the Heart of the American South

SeaRavenPress.com

THE CONFEDERATE MONUMENT

FRANKLIN, TENN.

Commemorating the Patriotism, Valor, and Sacrifice of the Confederate Soldier at the Battle of Franklin, Williamson County, Tenn., November 30, 1864

The Confederate Monument at Franklin, Tenn., memorializes the brave men who fought for the Conservative republic known as the Confederate States of America, one of the nicknames of the original U.S.A. In 1899 the monument was erected and paid for by private citizens, women's groups, and both Confederate and Union veterans—with the blessings of the local, state, and national government, as well as President William McKinley (a lifelong admirer of the Confederate soldier). Long may Franklin's Confederate Monument stand. It is the premier emblem of Americanism. See Appendix A. (Photo Lochlainn Seabrook)

INTRODUCTION

I have titled this book *The Battle of Franklin*. Technically, however, it should be called *The Battle of Franklin II*, for there were three major conflicts in this once small quiet village on the Harpeth River: Battle of Franklin I—April 10, 1863; Battle of Franklin II—November 30, 1864; Battle of Franklin III—December 17, 1864.[12] If this fact is little known and seldom discussed, we have a right to wonder what other important information has been left out of our history books pertaining to the Battle of Franklin. The answer is plenty!

(Photo Lochlainn Seabrook)

Most historians do not tell us, for instance, that at one point during Franklin II, as their Yankee commander was furiously calling them "cowards," hundreds of Union soldiers fled the field (considered by most governments to be an act of desertion, or at least dereliction of duty). We are also not told that Yankee soldiers often shot indiscriminately into the haze, *knowingly killing their own men*, and that after the conflict the Union army callously left its dead and wounded on the battlefield as it hurriedly marched north to Nashville under cover of darkness.

Another fact that is missing from our history books is the real reason behind the Confederacy's loss that day. Was it simply Confederate General John Bell Hood's outmoded military tactics, which could not compete with the "brilliant" strategies of Union General John McAllister Schofield? Hardly. According to a Confederate officer at the scene, it was due to the fact that "the Confederates were the attacking force, and the Federals were so well fortified as to render one man defending equal to about four attacking." This is military reality, without bias, emotion, opinion, or fabrication.

A host of other details are absent from the typical Civil War history, possibly an effort by regional historians to downplay Franklin while emphasizing the role and significance of other battles. Let us take casualty statistics, for example. Franklin's were horrific: with a 33 percent loss of infantrymen, this was the highest of any conflict of the War. In contrast, as just one illustration, during Pickett's celebrated charge at Gettysburg, long considered "the most devastating of the War," only 21 per cent were lost.

Additionally, Franklin marked the deaths of more general and field officers, and "in greater proportion to the numbers engaged," than in any Civil War battle: six general officers were killed, six wounded, and one captured, making a total of thirteen. As one Confederate officer wrote: "Thirteen regimental commanders were killed, thirty-two wounded, and nine captured. Besides these, many other field and line officers were killed and wounded, and about six thousand of the rank and file lay dead or disabled on the field at the close of that memorable day." Cleburne's Division alone suffered an almost unbelievable loss of 52 percent of its men; French's lost 45 percent, Walthall's 25 percent. Cheatham's Corps lost 35 percent of its soldiers.

(Photo Lochlainn Seabrook)

Such numbers have seldom if ever been recorded in any other conflict in world history. This truly makes the Battle of Franklin "the bloodiest of modern times," or as a Confederate colonel later noted: "In proportion to the number of officers who entered this conflict no other battle presents more terrible losses. For daring and desperate courage and mortality the battle of Franklin stands out as one of the most memorable conflicts of any war."

I side with my Confederate ancestors in claiming that at Franklin, "the bloodiest and most disastrous battle of the war was fought and won," not by the Union's numerical slaughter, as Yankees themselves still assert, but "by the bravery and self-sacrifice of the Confederate soldiers." Thus, while history has awarded the Liberal North the military victory, the Conservative South accords herself the moral victory.

(Photo Lochlainn Seabrook)

But what could possibly motivate so many Southerners, many of them boys in their teens, to give up their lives at Franklin, not to mention the War's 10,500 other battles and engagements? Our Left-wing authored history books tell us the South seceded and fought to "preserve slavery." But this could not be the reason, for the American abolition movement got its start in the South—and long before 1861. Also, both President Davis and President Lincoln repeatedly and emphatically stated that slavery had nothing to do with the War—as did the everyday Confederate and Union soldier.[13]

The answer, not surprisingly, is the most routinely disregarded fact of the entire War: *the two major parties were reversed in the mid 19th Century, making Davis and the Democrats Conservatives, Lincoln and the Republicans Liberals.* (They would not become the parties we know today until the 1896 election.)[14] Thus the "Civil War" was actually a major military struggle between Conservatives (the Confederates) and Liberals (the Union); the former fighting for conservatism (capitalist principles, constitutionalism, states rights, personal freedom, etc.), the latter fighting for liberalism (socialist principles, anti-constitutionalism, national supremacy, restricted personal freedom, etc.). To this day the South is still largely Conservative, the North is still primarily Liberal, vestiges of the Civil War era and beyond.

(Photo Lochlainn Seabrook)

What other vital information has been ignored, suppressed, or deleted from the history of the Battle of Franklin?

In the following pages the Confederate and Union soldiers who fought at "Tennessee's most handsomest town" in the Fall of 1864 answer this question; and, importantly, in words untouched by modern hands. This little book will thus help preserve *real history* (as opposed to the mainstream's *fake history*) for future generations. Our descendants deserve to know the Truth.

LOCHLAINN SEABROOK
Nashville, Tennessee, USA
October 2018
In Nobis Regnat Christus

BATTLE STATISTICS

NAME: The Battle of Franklin (II).

PRINCIPAL COMMANDERS: General John Bell Hood, C.S.A.; Major General John McAllister Schofield, U.S.A.

LOCATION: Franklin, Williamson County, Tennessee.

DATE: November 30, 1864.

PREVIOUS BATTLES: Columbia (November 24-29, 1864); Spring Hill (November 29, 1864).

SUBSEQUENT BATTLE: Nashville (December 15-16, 1864).

FORCES AT FRANKLIN: Army of Tennessee, C.S.A.: 19,000 men; 4th and 23rd Army Corps, Army of the Ohio and Cumberland, U.S.A.: 22,000 men.

ESTIMATED CASUALTIES: Stats according to C.S.A.: 6,300, C.S.A.; 8,326, U.S.A. Stats according to U.S.A.: 6,261, C.S.A.; 2,326, U.S.A. (All stats include captured, wounded, and missing.)

RESULTS: Union victory; Confederate power in the Western Theater substantially weakened.

General John Bell Hood (1831-1879), Confederate Commander at the Battle of Franklin.

General John M. Schofield (1831-1906), Union Commander at the Battle of Franklin.

Loyalty

to the truth of

Confederate history.

U.D.C. MOTTO, 1921

MAPS

Map showing Northern Alabama and Middle Tennessee, the region in which Hood's Tennessee Campaign took place in the Fall of 1864.

Union map showing travel routes and important locations of both armies between Columbia and Spring Hill, Tenn., in the latter half of November 1864—just prior to the Battle of Franklin.

General Hood's map of the Battle of Franklin.

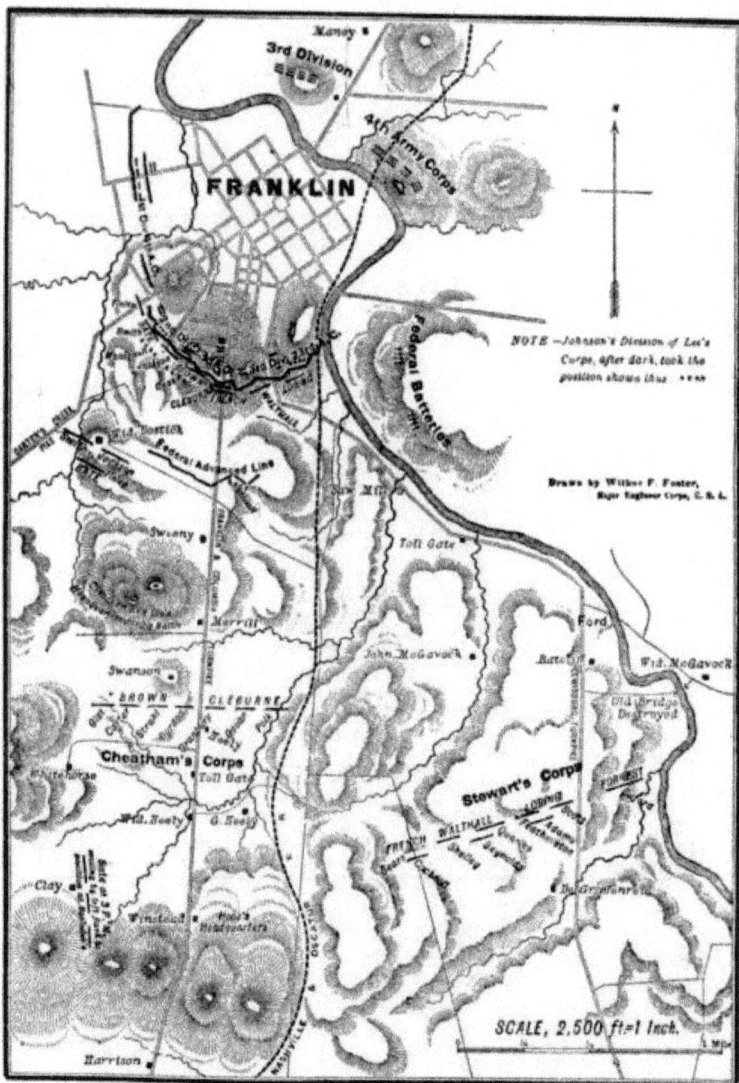

Confederate map of the Franklin battlefield, drawn up in 1885.

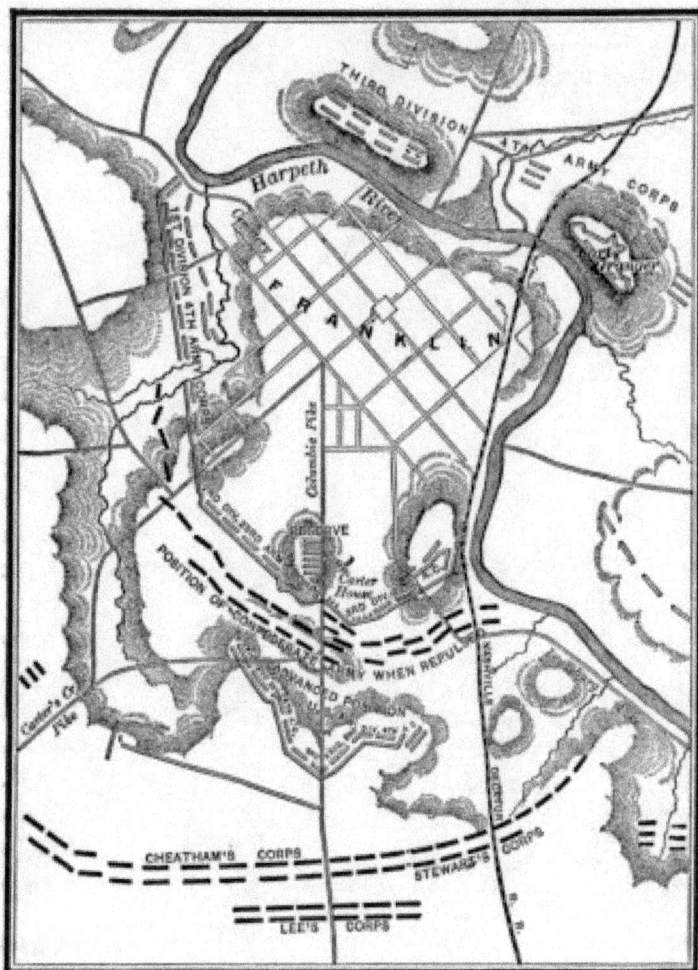

Union map of the Battle of Franklin.

Map of field works at Franklin as viewed by the Union.

SECTION 1

CONFEDERATE RECOLLECTIONS

"Nine times out of ten, when a man rose to fire, he fell back dead."

Confederate Recollections

GEN. HOOD'S DESCRIPTION OF THE BATTLE

☞ At early dawn [on November 30, 1864] the troops were put in motion in the direction of Franklin, marching as rapidly as possible to overtake the enemy before he crossed the Big Harpeth [River], eighteen miles from Spring Hill. Lieutenant General [Stephen Dill] Lee had crossed Duck river after dark the night previous, and, in order to reach Franklin, was obliged to march a distance of thirty miles. The head of his column arrived at Spring Hill at 9 a.m. on the 30th, and, after a short rest, followed in the wake of the main body.

A sudden change in sentiment here took place among officers and men: the Army [of Tennessee] became metamorphosed, as it were, in one night. A general feeling of mortification and disappointment pervaded its ranks. The troops appeared to recognize that a rare opportunity had been totally disregarded, and manifested, seemingly, a determination to retrieve, if possible, the fearful blunder of the previous afternoon and night [when, inexplicably, the Union army, under Gen. John M. Schofield, had been allowed to sneak past our encampment at Spring Hill]. The feeling existed which sometimes induces men who have long been wedded to but one policy to look beyond the sphere of their own convictions, and, at least, be willing to make trial of another course of action.

John B. Hood, C.S.A.

[Gen. Alexander P.] Stewart's Corps was first in order of march; [Gen. Benjamin F.] Cheatham followed immediately, and Lieutenant General Lee in rear. Within about three miles of Franklin, the enemy was discovered on the ridge over which passes the turnpike. As soon as the Confederate troops began to deploy, and skirmishers were thrown forward, the Federals withdrew slowly to the environs of the town.

It was about 3 p.m. when Lieutenant General Stewart moved to the right of the pike and began to establish his position in front of the enemy. Major General Cheatham's Corps, as it arrived in turn, filed off to the left of the road, and was also disposed in line of battle. The artillery was instructed to take no part in the engagement, on account of the danger to which women and children in the village would be exposed. General [Nathan B.] Forrest was ordered to post cavalry on both flanks, and, if the assault proved successful, to complete the ruin of the enemy by capturing those who attempted to escape in the direction of Nashville. Lee's Corps, as it arrived, was held in reserve, owing to the lateness of the hour and my inability, consequently, to post it on the extreme left. Schofield's position was rendered favorable for defence by open ground in front, and temporary entrenchments which the Federals had had time to throw up, notwithstanding the Confederate forces had marched in pursuit with all possible speed. At one or two points, along a short space, a slight abatis had been hastily constructed, by felling some small locust saplings in the vicinity.

Soon after Cheatham's Corps was massed on the left, Major General [Patrick R.] Cleburne came to me where I was seated on my horse in rear of the line, and asked permission to form his Division in two, or, if I remember correctly, three lines for the assault. I at once granted his request, stating that I desired the Federals to be driven into the river in their immediate rear and directing him to advise me as soon as he had completed the new disposition of his troops. Shortly afterward, Cheatham and Stewart reported all in readiness for action, and received orders to

A Franklin monument, as it looked around 1904, indicating where Gen. Cleburne fell. In the back left can be seen the Carter family's smoke house, which was in the line of battle. Around the monument are the scorched ruins of a school building, Battle Ground Academy (founded in 1889 and originally located near the cotton gin), which was destroyed by fire in 1902, and later rebuilt.

drive the enemy from his position into the river at all hazards. About that time Cleburne returned, and, expressing himself with an enthusiasm which he had never before betrayed in our intercourse, said, "General, I am ready, and have more hope in the final success of our cause than I have had at any time since the first gun was fired." I replied, "God grant it!" He turned and moved at once toward the head of his Division; a few moments thereafter, he was lost to my sight in the tumult of battle. These last words, spoken to me by this brave and distinguished soldier, I have often recalled; they can never leave my memory, as within forty minutes after he had uttered them, he lay lifeless upon or near the breastworks of the foe.

The two corps advanced in battle array at about 4 p.m., and soon swept away the first line of the Federals, who were driven back upon the main line. At this moment, resounded a concentrated roar of musketry, which recalled to me some of the deadliest struggles in Virginia, and which now proclaimed that the possession of Nashville was once more dependent upon the fortunes of war. The conflict continued to rage with intense fury; our troops succeeded in breaking the main line at one or more points, capturing and turning some of the guns on their opponents.

Just at this critical moment of the battle, a brigade of the enemy, reported to have been [Union Gen. David S.] Stanley's, gallantly charged, and restored the Federal line, capturing at the same time about one thousand of our troops within the entrenchments. Still the ground was obstinately contested, and, at several points upon the immediate sides of the breastworks, the combatants endeavored to use the musket upon one another, by inverting and raising it perpendicularly, in order to fire; neither antagonist, at this juncture, was able to retreat without almost a certainty of death. It was reported that soldiers were even dragged from one side of the breastworks to the other by men reaching over hurriedly and seizing their enemy by the hair or the collar.

"Neither antagonist, at this juncture, was able to retreat without almost a certainty of death."

Just before dark [Confederate Gen. Edward] Johnson's Division, of Lee's Corps, moved gallantly to the support of Cheatham; although it made a desperate charge and succeeded in capturing three stands of colors, it did not effect a permanent breach in the line of the enemy. The two remaining divisions could not unfortunately become engaged owing to the obscurity of night. The struggle continued with more or less violence until 9 p.m., when followed skirmishing and much desultory firing until about 3 a.m. the ensuing morning [December 1, 1864]. The enemy then withdrew, leaving his dead and wounded upon the field. Thus terminated one of the fiercest conflicts of the war.

Nightfall which closed in upon us so soon after the inauguration of the battle prevented the formation and participation of Lee's entire Corps on the extreme left. This, it may safely be asserted, saved Schofield's Army from destruction. I might, with equal assurance, assert that had Lieutenant General Lee been in advance at Spring Hill the previous afternoon, Schofield's Army never would have passed that point.

Shortly afterward I sent the following dispatch to the [C.S.] Secretary of War [James A. Seddon] and to [C.S.] General [Pierre G. T.] Beauregard: [No. 541.] "Headquarters, Six Miles to Nashville, December 3rd. — About 4 p.m., November 30th, we attacked the enemy at Franklin, and drove him from his outer line of temporary works into his interior line which he abandoned during the night, leaving his dead and wounded in our possession, and rapidly retreated to Nashville, closely pursued by our cavalry. We captured several stands of colors and about one thousand (1,000) prisoners. Our troops fought with great gallantry. We have to lament the loss of many gallant officers and brave men. Major General Cleburne, Brigadier Generals [States Rights] Gist, John Adams, [Otho F.] Strahl, and [Hiram B.] Granbury, were killed; Major General [John C.] Brown, Brigadier Generals [John C.] Carter [later died from his wounds], [Arthur M.] Manigault, [William A.] Quarles, [Francis M.] Cockrell, and [Thomas M.] Scott, were wounded, and Brigadier General [George W.] Gordon, captured. — J. B. Hood, General."

I rode over the scene of action the next morning, and could but indulge in sad and painful thought, as I beheld so many brave soldiers stricken down by the enemy whom, a few hours previous, at Spring Hill, we had held within the palm of our hands. The attack which entailed so great sacrifice of life, had, for reasons already stated, become a necessity as imperative as that which impelled General [Robert E.] Lee to order the assault at Gaines' Mill, when our troops charged across an open space, a distance of one mile, under a most galling fire of musketry and artillery, against an enemy heavily entrenched. The heroes in that action fought not more gallantly than the soldiers of the Army of Tennessee upon the field of Franklin. These had been gloriously led by their officers, many of whom had fallen either upon or near the Federal breastworks, dying as the brave should prefer to die, in the intense and exalted excitement of battle.

Major General Cleburne had been distinguished for his admirable conduct upon many fields, and his loss, at this moment, was irreparable. In order to estimate fully the value of his services at this particular juncture, I will, in a few words, advert to our past relations. He was a man of equally quick perception and strong character, and was,

Patrick R. Cleburne, C.S.A.

especially in one respect, in advance of many of our people. He possessed the boldness and the wisdom to earnestly advocate, at an early period of the war, the freedom of the negro and the enrollment [in the Confederate military] of the young and able-bodied men of that race. This stroke of policy and additional source of strength to our Armies, would, in my opinion, have given us our independence.[15] He was for the first time under my immediate command at New Hope Church where his Division, formed for action according to my specific instructions, achieved the most brilliant success of Johnston's campaign. He had full knowledge of all the circumstances and difficulties which attended the battles of the 20th, and 22nd of July. It will be remembered that he called at my headquarters after these two engagements, and communicated to me [Confederate Gen. William J.] Hardee's unfortunate words of caution to the troops, in regard to breastworks, just before the battle of the 20th. He knew also in what manner my orders at Spring Hill had been totally disregarded.

After our last brief interview which was followed so quickly by his [Cleburne's] death, I sought to account for his sudden revolution of feeling and his hopefulness, since he had been regarded as not over sanguine of the final triumph of our cause. I formed the conviction that he became satisfied on the morning of the 30th of November, after having reviewed the occurrences of the previous afternoon and night, and those of the 20th and 22nd of July, that I was not the reckless, indiscreet commander the [Joseph E.] Johnston-[Louis]Wigfall party represented me; that I had been harshly judged, and feebly sustained by the officers and men; that I was dealing blows and making moves which had at least the promise of happy results, and that we should have achieved decided success on two occasions around Atlanta as well as at Spring Hill. He therefore made a sudden and firm resolution to support me in all my operations, believing that my movements and manner of handling troops were based upon correct principles. It has been said he stated, upon the morning after the affair of Spring Hill, that he would never again allow one of my orders for battle to be disobeyed, if he could prevent it. For these reasons his loss became doubly great to me. The heroic career and death of this distinguished soldier must ever endear the memory of his last words to his commander, and should entitle his name to be inscribed in immortal characters in the annals of our history.

A similar revolution in feeling took place to a great extent among both officers and men, the morning of the day upon which was fought the battle of Franklin; this change—and in a measure the improved morale of the Army, which had resulted from a forward movement of one hundred and eighty miles—occasioned the extraordinary gallantry and desperate fighting witnessed on that field.

The subjoined extract from Van Horne's *History of the Army of the Cumberland*, will confirm my assertion in regard to our nearly-won victory. Referring to the main breach in the Federal works, the author says: "Toward the breach, the enemy's heavy central lines began to press, and to his lateral lines were turned, in seemingly overwhelming convergence. To General Hood, the advantage so easily gained, premised the capture or destruction

Stephen D. Lee, C.S.A.

of the National [Union] Army, and he and his Army were inspired to quickest action to maintain and utilize it for this grand achievement. And he certainly could have maintained his hold of the National line, and used for extreme success, had time been given him to thrust into the breach his rapidly advancing and massive rear lines; and as it was, he began to gain ground, right and left, from the Columbia road."

As shown by Colonel Mason's official report, made on the 10th of December [1864], ten days after the battle, our effective strength was: Infantry, eighteen thousand three hundred and forty-two (18,342); artillery, two thousand four hundred and five (2,405); cavalry, two thousand three hundred and six (2,306); total, twenty-three thousand and fifty-three (23,053). This last number, subtracted from thirty thousand six hundred (30,600), the strength of the Army at Florence, shows a total loss from all causes of seven thousand five hundred and forty seven (7,547), from the 6th of November to the 10th of December, which period includes the engagements at Columbia, Franklin, and of Forrest's cavalry.

The enemy's estimate of our losses as well as of the number of Confederate colors captured is erroneous, as will be seen by the following telegram: [No. 560.] "Headquarters near Nashville, on Franklin Pike, December 15th, 1864. — Honorable J. A. Seddon, Secretary of War, Richmond. The enemy claim that we lost thirty colors in the fight at Franklin. We lost thirteen, capturing nearly the same number. The men who bore ours were killed on or within the enemy's interior line of works. J. B. Hood, General."

The estimate of the actual loss at Franklin, given in my official report, was made with the assistance of [Confederate] General [Francis A.] Shoup, my chief of staff, and is, I consider, correct. However, I will estimate later the total loss from all causes, in order to avoid possible error.

After the failure of my cherished plan to crush Schofield's Army before it reached its strongly fortified position around Nashville, I remained with an effective force of only twenty-three thousand and fifty-three. I was therefore well aware of our inability to attack the Federals in their new stronghold with any hope of success, although

"The Yanks abandoned the field at Franklin, leaving their dead and wounded in our possession."

Schofield's troops had abandoned the field at Franklin, leaving their dead and wounded in our possession, and had hastened with considerable alarm into their fortifications—which latter information, in regard to their condition after the battle, I obtained through spies. I knew equally well that in the absence of the prestige of complete victory, I could not venture with my small force to cross the Cumberland river into Kentucky, without first receiving reinforcements from the Trans-Mississippi Department. I felt convinced that the Tennesseans and Kentuckians would not join our forces, since we had failed in the first instance to defeat the Federal Army and capture Nashville. The President [Davis] was still urgent in his instructions relative to the transference of troops to the Army of Tennessee from Texas, and I daily hoped to receive the glad tidings of their safe passage across the Mississippi river.

Thus, unless strengthened by these long-looked for reinforcements, the only remaining chance of success in the campaign, at this juncture, was to take position, entrench around Nashville, and await [Union General George H.] Thomas's attack which, if handsomely repulsed, might afford us an opportunity to follow up our advantage on the spot, and enter the city on the heels of the enemy.

I could not afford to turn southward, unless for the special purpose of forming a junction with the expected reinforcements from Texas, and with the avowed intention to march back again upon Nashville. In truth, our Army was in that condition which rendered it more judicious the men should face a decisive issue rather than retreat—in other words, rather than renounce the honor of their cause, without having made a last and manful effort to lift up the sinking fortunes of the Confederacy.

George H. Thomas, U.S.A.

I therefore determined to move upon Nashville, to entrench, to accept the chances of reinforcements from Texas, and, even at the risk of an attack in the meantime by overwhelming numbers, to adopt the only feasible means of defeating the enemy with my reduced numbers, viz., to await his attack, and, if favored by success, to follow him into his works. I was apprised of each accession to Thomas's Army, but was still unwilling to abandon the ground as long as I saw a shadow of probability of assistance from the Trans-Mississippi Department, or of victory in battle; and, as I have just remarked, the troops would, I believed, return better satisfied even after defeat if, in grasping at the last straw, they felt that a brave and vigorous effort had been made to save the country from disaster [that is, the imposition of Yankee Liberal rule in the South]. Such, at the time, was my opinion, which I have since had no reason to alter.

In accordance with these convictions, I ordered the Army to move forward on the 1st of December in the direction of Nashville; Lee's Corps marched in advance, followed by Stewart's and Cheatham's Corps, and the troops bivouacked that night in the vicinity of Brentwood. On the morning of the 2nd, the march was resumed, and line of battle formed in front of Nashville. Lee's Corps was placed in the centre and across the Franklin pike; Stewart occupied the left, and Cheatham the right—their flanks extending as near the Cumberland as possible, whilst Forrest's cavalry filled the gap between them and the river.[16] — CONFEDERATE GENERAL JOHN BELL HOOD (Army of Tennessee)

REPORT FROM A FUTURE TENNESSEE GOVERNOR

☞ At daylight [November 30, 1864] Cheatham's corps passed through the village of Spring Hill, and between 1 and 2 o'clock p.m. the army [of Tennessee, C.S.A.] reached the vicinity of Franklin, and Stewart's and Cheatham's corps were put in positions. The enemy was heavily intrenched and was superior in numbers and equipment. On the morning of the battle, General Schofield, commanding the Federal army, had behind his works 23,734 infantry and artillery, and his cavalry numbered 5,500. Maj.-Gen. Jacob D. Cox, U.S.A., upon whose authority these figures are given, states . . . that Hood delivered the assault on the Federal lines with "two or three hundred less than 24,000" men, and gives Forrest's strength at 9,000. Maj.-Gen. John C. Brown [C.S.A.] reported that on the morning of November 29, 1864, he had not exceeding 2,750 men in his division, the largest in Cheatham's corps, and the three divisions did not exceed 6,000.

Benjamin F. Cheatham, C.S.A.

Smith's brigade of Cleburne's division was not present. Stewart's corps after Allatoona was less than 7,000, and with Johnson's division of Lee's corps, the assaulting column did not exceed 16,000 men. General Forrest stated in his official report that the entire cavalry force under his command was about 5,000.

[William B.] Bate's division was on the left, Brown's in the center, Cleburne's on the right. General Bate says his line "charged the works of the enemy. My right got to the works (the second line) and remained there until morning; the left was driven back. The enemy's works were strong and defiant, constructed on a slight elevation, with few obstructions in front for several hundred yards. The works to the left of Carter's creek turnpike were not strong, and with a vigorous assault should have been carried; a fact, however, not known until next day." Bate's division sustained a loss of 47 killed and 253 wounded. Capt. Tod Carter, on staff duty with Smith's Tennessee brigade, fell mortally wounded near the enemy's works and almost at the door of his father's house.

No more magnificent spectacle was ever witnessed than the advance of the two divisions commanded by Cleburne and Brown; no two divisions of the army were ever led with greater skill and gallantry; no generals of division were ever supported with better ability by brigade, regimental and company officers. The troops were veterans who had never failed to respond to orders, although discouraged by recent and frequent disasters; and fully alive to the desperation of the assault about to be made, they advanced with noble courage. Before troops of equal numbers in the open field they would have been irresistible, but to attack intrenched troops, superior in numbers, advancing over an open plain without cover, was a disregard of the rules of war, a waste of precious lives, and a wrecking of an army once the pride and hope of the Southwest.

John C. Brown, C.S.A.

Major-General Stanley, commanding the Fourth Federal corps, in his official report stated that: "In view of the strong position we held, nothing appeared so improbable as that they [the Confederates] would assault. I felt so confident in this belief that I did not leave General Schofield's headquarters until the firing commenced." Major-General Cox, commanding the Twenty-third corps, and in active command of the Federal line of battle, undertakes to account for the attack made by General Hood thus: "His exasperation at what he regarded as a hair's breadth escape on our part from the toils in which he thought he had encompassed us at Spring Hill had probably clouded his judgment. He blamed some of his subordinates for the hesitation which he seems himself to have been responsible for, and now, in an excitement which led him astray, he determined to risk everything upon a desperate assault." The same eminent author, referring to the assault made by Cleburne and Brown on the Federal center, says: "They were seen coming in splendid array. The sight was one to send a thrill through the heart, and those who saw it have never forgotten its martial magnificence."

[Confederate] Maj.-Gen. John C. Brown, in a report to General Cheatham of the operations of his command, said: "After we had dislodged the enemy's advance pickets from the chain of ridges in front of Franklin, Generals Bate and Cleburne and myself were summoned to the commanding general at a point very near the Columbia turnpike road, and, as I recollect, both yourself and General Stewart were present. From that point we had an unobstructed view of the enemy's works in front of Franklin, across the turnpike road, and for some distance to the right and left. My position was immediately on the left of the turnpike, while Cleburne was upon the right. General Bate's position was either in my rear or immediately upon my left.

"The commanding general [Hood], after surveying the field, remarked in substance, 'The country around Franklin for many miles is open and exposed to the full view of the Federal army, and I cannot mask the movements of my troops so as to turn either flank of the enemy, and if I attempt it he will withdraw and precede me into Nashville. While his immediate center is very strong, his flanks are weak. Stewart's corps is massed in [John] McGavock's woods on the right, and I will send Bate's division under cover of the hills to the left in advance of the movement of my center; giving him time sufficient to get into position to attack concurrently with the center column. He can connect with Chalmers' right (posted upon the Harpeth [River] below Franklin) and with Brown's left.' The policy of General Hood's decision was not discussed, and I cannot recollect any question propounded by him to any one present indicating a desire for an expression of opinion by any one. He thereupon ordered Bate to move at once, and directed Stewart to attack with his corps the enemy's left flank. Cleburne and myself were directed to form in conjunction, Cleburne on the right and I on the left of the turnpike, and threaten and (if not routed before we reached the works) attack the enemy's center; but were instructed not to move until further orders from him, as he desired Bate and Stewart, having a longer distance to march, to move in advance of us.

"After the expiration of half an hour or more, at a signal from yourself, Cleburne and myself were directed to commence our movement. We advanced our line, attacking simultaneously the enemy's front line of works (being a lunette some 400 or 500 yards in advance of the main works). We routed and drove that line back upon the enemy's main line with but slight loss to ourselves and without impeding the advance of our line. General Cleburne and myself met several times upon the turnpike road and conferred and acted in harmony in the movement. When we assaulted the main line, we carried the works in many places. General Gordon, commanding the right brigade of my front line, stormed and carried the enemy's works at the turnpike road and advanced a

George W. Gordon, C.S.A.

considerable distance within the works, when he and a part of his command were captured. The enemy rapidly reinforced his center from his flanks, and the slaughter in our ranks was frightful, considering the very short time in which we were engaged. The loss was so heavy to my front line that I immediately brought forward the supporting brigades (Strahl's and Carter's), and we held the works in a hand-to-hand fight, with varying fortune, until night closed upon the bloody conflict. The engagement lasted but little more than one hour, during which time the fire of the enemy's infantry was terrific. Generals Gist and Strahl were killed on the field, with nearly all of their staff officers. General Carter received a mortal wound from which he died in a few hours. When I was shot from my horse near nightfall, I had only one staff officer and two couriers on duty.

John C. Carter, C.S.A.

"General Carter, whose command was on my extreme left, reported to me once through a member of his staff, and again in person, that there were no supports on his left and that flank was being threatened, and on personal inspection I found that there were no troops on my left at sunset. I regret very much that the loss of my papers will not allow me to give you in detail the list of casualties and to mention the conduct of very many officers and men conspicuous for their gallantry during the engagement. It is just to say, however, that the entire command did its full duty. The enemy were intrenched in strong works protected in front by an abatis of black locust, which was almost impassable, and our advancing lines were met by successive volleys of musketry that would have repulsed any but well-tried and dauntless veterans."

Gist's and Gordon's brigades reached the outer ditch of the intrenchments, mounted the works and met the enemy in a death struggle. The colors of the Twenty-fourth South Carolina, says its gallant Col. Ellison Capers, were planted and defended on the parapet. Part of both brigades went over the works, General Gordon himself was captured, and Col. Horace Rice, Eleventh and Twenty-ninth Tennessee (consolidated), was wounded inside of the enemy's main line. General Gordon states that "the gallant Ensign-Sergeant Drew, of the Twenty-ninth, bearing the flag of the Eleventh, was killed as he mounted the main line of works, fell inside and died upon his colors, upon whose folds are still seen marks of his blood."

Lieut. James A. Tillman, Twenty-fourth South Carolina, led his company over the works and captured 40 prisoners and the colors of the

Ninety-seventh Ohio, this being the only stand of colors captured by the Confederate forces. General Gist, gallant gentleman and soldier, was killed in the advance; Colonel Capers was dangerously, and his lieutenant-colonel, J. S. Jones, mortally wounded. The loss of officers and men in Gist's brigade was very great. On the march

The Harrison House, Franklin, Tenn., where Confederate Gen. John C. Carter died of his wounds several days after the Battle of Franklin. (Photo Lochlainn Seabrook)

to Nashville it was commanded by Captain Gillis, Forty-sixth Georgia. Its senior officer, Colonel Capers, recovered and received a well-earned promotion. At the close of hostilities between the States, he dedicated himself to the church, and in that sacred calling has won eminence and the love of his people.

Cheatham's division was commanded after the battle by the gallant Col. C. C. Hurt, Ninth Tennessee, Gen. John C. Brew being dangerously wounded. Brig.-Gen. John C. Carter was mortally wounded, Gist and Strahl were killed, Gordon was captured inside the enemy's works. Majs. John Ingram and Thomas F. Henry and Capt. M. B. Pilcher of the division staff were severely wounded; Maj. Joseph Vaulx, always gallant and reliable, alone escaped unhurt. No division of the army ever sustained such a loss in general officers.

O. F. Strahl was born on the banks of the Muskingum [River in Ohio], came to Tennessee in his youth, and was as thoroughly identified with the State as any one of her sons. He gave to the Fourth Tennessee its drill and discipline, and made it a noted regiment; and, succeeding A. P. Stewart in command of his brigade, added splendor to the reputation won for it by that accomplished soldier. When General Strahl entered upon the Tennessee campaign he was just recovering from a dangerous wound received at the battle of Atlanta on the 22nd of July. He was a very accomplished tactician, and always handled his regiment and brigade with ease and skill. He was most fortunate in his subordinates, with officers like Col. Andrew J. Keller; Col. A. D. Gwynne, distinguished at Mill Creek Gap, and called by his comrades the "Knight of Gwynne"; Lieut.-Col. Luke W. Finlay, severely wounded at Shiloh, Perryville and New Hope church, and Maj. Henry Hampton, dangerously wounded at Perryville. The officers of his staff, Captain Johnston, adjutant-general, Lieut. John H. Marsh, inspector general, soldiers of experience and gallantry, were both killed.

John C. Carter was a native of Georgia, a citizen of Tennessee, where he was educated, entered the service as a lieutenant in the Thirty-eighth Tennessee, won honorable mention from his colonel at Shiloh, and further promotion and honor until he was made a brigadier-general. He early attracted the attention of his division general, upon whose recommendation his final advancement was made upon his merit. He had a wonderful gentleness of manner, coupled with a dauntless courage. Every field officer of his brigade except Colonel Hurt was killed, wounded or captured on the enemy's works. In one regiment, the gallant Sixth, Orderly-Sergt. W. H. Bruner remained the ranking officer.

Gen. William A. Quarles, of Tennessee, was dangerously wounded and captured. His division general, Walthall, said of him: "Brigadier-General Quarles was severely wounded at the head of his brigade within a short distance of the enemy's inner line, and all his staff officers on duty [W. B. Munford and Capt. S. A. Conley] were killed." Col. Isaac N. Holme, Forty-second Tennessee, and Capt. R. T. Johnson, Forty-ninth, were severely wounded; Lieut.-Col. T. M. Atkins, Forty-ninth, Maj. S. C. Cooper, Forty-sixth, and Capt. James J. Rittenburg, Fifty-third, were wounded and captured, and Maj. J. E. McDonald, Fifty-fifth, and Capt. R. T. Coulter, were killed, leaving a captain in command of the brigade.

William A. Quarles, C.S.A.

Brig.-Gen. John Adams, of Tennessee, was killed after leading his command up to the enemy's main line of works. [Union] Gen. Jacob D. Cox says of him: "In one of the lulls between these attacks, when the smoke was so thick that one could see a very little way in front, the officers of the line discovered a mounted officer in front forming for another attack or rallying them after a repulse. Shots were fired and horse and rider both fell. The horse struggled to his feet and dashed for the breastworks, leaped upon it and fell dead astride it. The wounded officer was Gen. John Adams. He was brought in and soon died."

General Hood reported the loss of the army of Tennessee at 4,500. The loss of Schofield's army numbered 8,326 killed, wounded and missing. Of this number, 1,104 were captured by the Confederates, about 600 of them by Brown and Cleburne from the enemy's line in advance of his intrenchments.

Gen. J. D. Cox says the Federal loss in killed was "trifling everywhere but near the center," the point assailed by Cleburne and Brown. No report with list of casualties was ever made, and no data exist for the ascertainment of the actual losses of these two divisions, but it must have been 40 per cent in killed, wounded and missing. In Quarles' Tennessee brigade of Stewart's corps, the loss was just as great, and the death rate in Stewart's and Cheatham's corps was out of the usual proportion. It was great enough to make Tennessee a land of mourning.

The attacks of the Confederates were repeated at intervals until dark, and on part of the line until 9 o'clock. At midnight the Federal forces were withdrawn and marched to Nashville.

After our dead comrades were buried and the wounded of both armies provided for, the army of Tennessee moved forward to the front of

James D. Porter, C.S.A.

Nashville, where on the 2nd of December a line of battle was formed and intrenchments provided.[17] — CONFEDERATE OFFICER JAMES DAVIS PORTER (on the staff of Gen. Benjamin F. Cheatham)

ADDRESS BY THE COMMANDER-IN-CHIEF OF THE UCV

☛ Five and thirty years ago to-day there occurred upon yonder field one of the most dramatic and sanguinary conflicts recorded in the annals of warfare. If we give first an account of the battle, it will enable us to understand more fully the matchless prowess and splendid heroism of the brave and patriotic men who fell upon this field, and whose memories and deeds we honor to-day.

About 2 o'clock in the afternoon of that tragic and memorable day the Confederate army, commanded by Gen. J. B. Hood, appeared near the crest of yon range of hills that looks down from the South upon this beautiful valley, but not in view of the Federal army, commanded by Gen. Schofield, that then encircled your devoted little city as a huge anaconda. The Confederate army was halted near the southern crest of the hills, and was kept under cover thereof, preparatory to making dispositions for battle, until about 4 o'clock.

In the meantime the Confederate officers had been inspecting the enemy's position with field glasses, and had discovered that he was fortified immediately south of the town, and extending to the east and west—his wings apparently resting on the stream that bounds the town in an abrupt bend on the north. About this time (4 o'clock) Gens. Hood and Cheatham rode to where Gen. Brown and his brigade commanders were, the speaker among the number, where the Columbia pike crosses the hills coming north. After they had examined the enemy's position from that point, Gen. Hood said to Cheatham: "General, get your command ready to go at the work immediately; we have no time to lose. Tell your officers to go with the men, to stop at nothing, and to sweep everything before them." Gen. Cheatham turned to us and said: "Gentlemen, you have heard Gen. Hood's orders. Get your commands ready to move forward immediately." The speaker had examined the enemy's position with a strong field glass, and had discovered that his defenses of earthworks were formidable, especially in the vicinity of where the pike leading into the town crossed them; and when he heard Gen. Hood's orders to sweep everything before us he felt that a desperate and death-dealing struggle was about to ensue. And it was.

I had observed that, in addition to the enemy's main and rear line of fortifications, there was, from six to eight hundred paces in front of that, another line of works, but extending only two or three hundred paces on each side of the pike leading into the town, and that this short and isolated line was well manned. So that in our immediate front (Cheatham's right brigade and Cleburne's left) two lines of fortifications had to be stormed and taken if we were victorious.

Our commands were promptly moved into the positions. Brown's Division of Cheatham's Corps formed to the left of the pike leading into Franklin, with his right wing resting on the pike, which was to be his right guide in moving to the assault. Cleburne's Division was formed on the right of the pike mentioned, with his left wing resting thereon. The brigade formation of Brown's Division was Gist's and Gordon's Brigades in the front line—Gordon on the right, Gist on the left—Gordon's right wing resting on the pike. Carter's and Strahl's Brigades formed the second line of battle in this division—Carter supporting Gist and Strahl supporting Gordon—the supporting lines being ordered to keep within two hundred paces of the front line. Bate's Division was moved to the left of Brown's, thus making the formation of Cheatham's Corps: Cleburne's Division on the right, Brown's in the center, and Bate's on the left. Gen. Stewart's Corps was on the right of Cheatham's. Only one division of Lee's Corps (Johnson's) had arrived, and that was held in reserve.

William B. Bate, C.S.A.

When these dispositions were made the advance was ordered. We were—one and a fourth to one and a half miles away on the elevation of hills that looked down upon the then solemn and tranquil valley—to begin the charge in a regimental movement that our tactics designated, "double column at half distance," in order that we might move with more facility and precision, and also more easily pass obstacles, such as fences and small groves of trees that here and there interspersed the otherwise open plain upon which the mighty struggle was soon to take place.

In describing the battle I can speak only from personal knowledge of the action of the men and officers near me in the fight.

As the array of columns which has been mentioned, with a front of two or more miles in length, moved steadily down the heights into the valley below, with flying banners, beating drums, and bristling guns, it presented the most magnificent and spectacular military pageant ever witnessed by that veteran army, or perhaps any other during that great international war. It presented a scene so imposing and thrilling in its grandeur that the sense of ensuing danger was lost in the sublime emotions inspired by the surpassing martial panorama.

"As the array of columns moved steadily down the heights into the valley below, with flying banners, beating drums, and bristling guns, it presented the most magnificent and spectacular military pageant ever witnessed by that veteran army."

When we had arrived within four or five hundred paces of the enemy's first and short line of intrenchments our columns were deployed from the march into two lines of battle, and were halted for a few moments and aligned, preparatory to the charge upon this line. The speaker here dismounted to charge with the men on foot.

Immediately after the alignment just mentioned was made the "charge" was ordered, and, with an impetuous rush and a startling shout, we dashed wildly forward on this line. The enemy delivered one volley at our rushing ranks and precipitately fled for refuge to his rear and main line of defense. When they fled the shout was raised by some one of the charging Confederates: "Go into the works with them! Go into the works with them!" This cry was quickly caught up and wildly vociferated from a thousand straining throats as we rushed on after the flying forces we had routed—killing some in our running fire, capturing others who were slow of foot, and sustaining but little loss ourselves until, perhaps, within a hundred paces of their main line and stronghold, when it seemed to me that hell itself had exploded in our faces. Men fell right and left, fast and thick, and the field was covered at this point with a mantle of dead and dying men.

They had thus long reserved their fire for the safety of their routed comrades, who were fleeing to them for protection, and who were just in front of and mingled with our pursuing forces. When it was no longer safe for those in the works to reserve their fire to protect their comrades they opened upon us (regardless of their own men, with whom we had mingled in the run) such a storm of shot and shell, canister and musketry, that the very air was hideous with the terrifying shrieks of the mad messengers of death. The booming of cannons, the bursting of bombs, the screaming of shells, the rattle of musketry, the shouting of the combatants, and the falling of men—all made a scene of surpassing terror and appalling grandeur. "Such a din was there, as if men fought on earth below, and fiends in upper air." It yet seems a mystery and a wonder how any of us ever reached the works alive.

Amidst this scene Gen. Cleburne came charging from our left, through his men and mine, diagonally toward the enemy's works, looking like a war god in a battle picture. His horse, running with great speed, would have plunged over and trampled the speaker to the ground if he had not

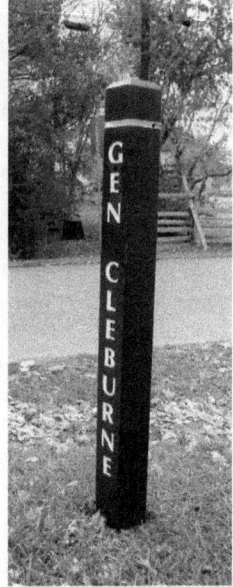

Wooden marker, Franklin, Tenn., indicating where Gen. Cleburne fell and died during the battle. (Photo Lochlainn Seabrook)

checked his own pace as he ran on foot to let the charger pass. This was near the works, and Gen. Cleburne must have fallen immediately after this, though I saw him no more.

On we rushed, Granbury's men and mine mingling as we approached the enemy's works, on reaching which the most of us halted in the ditch on the outside, amid the dead and dying men of both armies. From the time the enemy opened the fire they had reserved so long they slew friend and foe alike. We reached the works with but few men, and these were well-nigh exhausted, having charged at full speed for more than half a mile. Some of our comrades in their impetuosity went over the works at this point, but were clubbed to the earth with musketry or pierced with bayonets. But, as stated, the most of our small number halted in the ditch on the outside, seeing that it was futile death to attempt to overcome, in a hand-to-hand struggle, such superior numbers, especially in our exhausted condition. So we did not break the line at this point. But for quite a while, however, we fought them across their breastworks, both sides lying low and putting their guns under the head-logs that were on the earthworks, firing nervously, rapidly, and at random, and not exposing any part of the body except the hand that fired the gun. While this melee, which now seems like a hideous dream, was going on across the works we were exposed to a dangerous and destructive enfilading fire of the enemy on our left, there being an angle in their works; and also to the fire of some of our own forces of Gen. Stewart's Command from our right rear, there being another angle in the works in that direction. Our position at the works was just to the left of the famous old ginhouse, between that and the pike—some of my men and myself, in the rush and confusion, having crossed to Cleburne's side of the pike, reached the works with some of Granbury's men.

Finally, the fatality to us, as we crouched and fought in the ditch, became so great from these three fires—front, left, and rear—that some of the men shouted to the enemy across the line that if they would "cease firing" they would surrender. Amid the uproar this was not heard, and a signal of surrender was made by putting our hats or caps on our bayonets fixed on our guns and holding them up above the works. The first of these signals that were seen were perforated by the enemy's bullets. I suppose they thought it was our heads, or they did not know what it meant. At length, however, they heard and understood our men, and, amid the fearful din, we distinctly heard the command, "Cease firing!"

The oft-mentioned cotton ginhouse (long since disappeared), Franklin, Tenn., epicenter of the battle.

given on the other side of the works; and in a moment more all was comparatively quiet in our immediate front, and the men walked over the works and surrendered. It was fatal to leave the ditch and attempt to escape to the rear. Every man who attempted it—and a number did—was at once shot down. I ordered them to remain in the ditch until I told them they could surrender. When all had walked over the works except one of my men and myself he asked if I was not going over. I replied in the negative, saying that I would remain under cover of the dead in the ditch until night, which was approaching. He said he would remain with me. But the bullets from our right rear and the enfilading fire on our left (and which had never ceased) fell so thickly about us that I finally said, "We shall be killed if we remain here," at the same time handing him a white handkerchief and telling him to put it on his bayonet and walk over the works. He did so, and I followed him.

As I jumped down on the inside of the works a Federal soldier struck at my head with the butt of his gun; but the stroke was averted from my head by another Federal soldier pushing the gun as it came down, causing it to give me only a glancing blow upon the shoulder, saying as he did so: "Don't strike him. He is surrendering." I was immediately placed in charge of two soldiers, who were ordered to hurry me to the rear. There was great confusion, not to say consternation, in the enemy's ranks, even after we surrendered. I heard officers cursing their men and saw them striking them with their swords to hold them at the works. And when I arrived, in charge of the escort mentioned, at the pontoon bridge across [the] Harpeth River, about a half mile from where I was captured, I saw hundreds of stragglers from the Federal army huddled and attempting to cross the stream, but were kept back by officers with drawn swords and pistols, who were urging them to return to the field they had abandoned.

Reverting again to the battle, I remark that the main line of the enemy's defenses was broken by the left of Gordon's Brigade, under the splendid leadership of Col. Horace Rice, commanding his (the Twenty-Ninth) and my old regiment (the Eleventh Tennessee Infantry) consolidated, some of the soldiers being killed fifty or more paces within the enemy's line, Col. Rice himself being wounded after he had crossed the works. But at this critical juncture, and before the rout could be made general, Opdyckes's Brigade of Federal reenforcements arrived at the critical moment in front of Rice with the small force he was leading, and pressed them back to the works they had taken, but which they held till the Federals retreated during the night.

Col. Frank A. Burr, an ex-Federal soldier and a brilliant writer, in an account of this battle, published in 1883, gives me the credit of leading the men who

The Harpeth River, Franklin, Tenn. (Photo Lochlainn Seabrook)

broke the main line of the Federal defenses, but I am not entitled to this honor. It belongs to my friend and comrade and colonel, Horace Rice, long since dead. The gallant ensign of this consolidated regiment, Serg. Dru, leading the charge, sprang upon the works, was shot down, and fell inside of the line, with this standard in his hand. [Gen. Gordon here shows his audience the battle flag of the Eleventh Tennessee Infantry.] This dark discoloration which we see is the blood of that martyr, Serg. Dru, who fell and died upon it. These tattered fragments, these bullet holes, and this faded blood speak a more eloquent and glorious history for that regiment than all the eulogies that my poor tongue can utter. I do not exhibit this flag and speak thus so much to individualize heroic deeds and special commands as to indicate the general prowess, courage, and self-sacrifice that characterized the action of that valiant, war-worn, and battle-scarred army known in history as the Army of Tennessee. Other flags were perforated and other commands decimated on that momentous day, other deeds performed that deserve equal and honorable mention.

The opposing forces in this battle were nearly equal in numbers, the Confederates having about 19,000 infantry actually engaged and the Federals about 22,000. But, as already stated, the Confederates were the attacking force, and the Federals were so well fortified as to render one man defending equal to about four attacking.

The casualties in this battle were appalling, especially on the Confederate side. In general and field officers, especially, they were greater in proportion to numbers engaged than in any battle of the war. Six general officers were killed, six wounded, and one captured—total, thirteen. Of the four brigadier generals of Brown's Division, Carter, Gist, and Strahl were killed and Gordon captured, and Maj. Gen. Brown severely wounded;

States Rights Gist, C.S.A.

so that this division was commanded next day by a colonel. Maj. Gen. Cleburne and Brig. Gen. Granbury, of his division, were killed. Maj. Gen. John Adams, of Gen. Stewart's Corps, was killed, himself and horse falling upon the enemy's works. Gens. Cockrell, Quarles, Scott, Manigault, and one other general officer, whose name I cannot now recall, were wounded. Thirteen regimental commanders were killed, thirty-two wounded, and nine captured. Besides these, many other field and line officers were killed and wounded, and about six thousand of the rank and file lay dead or disabled on the field at the close of that memorable day. The Federal loss, I think, was about one-third as great as the Confederate. The infantry forces actually engaged lost 33 per cent. In Stewart's Corps the loss was 28 per cent; in Cheatham's, 35 percent. The loss in Stewart's Corps by divisions was: Loring's, 23; Walthall's, 25, and French's, 45 per cent. In Cheatham's Corps, by divisions, the loss was: Bate's, 16; Brown's, 31; and Cleburne's, 52 per cent. In Loring's Corps, Johnson's Division (the only division of this corps that was in the battle and in the second charge), the loss was 21 per cent.

In Forrest's Cavalry Corps, which did valiant service, the loss in Jackson's and Chalmers's Divisions was 5 per cent. Pickett's Division, in its famous charge at Gettysburg, lost 21 per cent, while the loss in this battle (Franklin) of the entire infantry engaged was 33 per cent, or 12 per cent greater than that of Pickett at Gettysburg. Military statistics of foreign and American battles, as compiled by Lieut. Col. Dodge, of the United States army, show the following losses: Prussians, up to Waterloo, in eight battles, 18 2-5 per cent; at Konniggratz, nearly 4 per cent. Austrians, up to Waterloo, in seven battles, 11 1-5 percent; since, in two, 8 1-2 per cent. French, up to Waterloo, in nine battles, 22 2-5 per cent; since, in nine, nearly 9 per cent. Germans, since 1745, in eight battles, 11 1-2 per cent. English, in four battles, nearly 10 2-5 per cent. Federals, in eleven battles, nearly 13 per cent. Confederates, in eleven battles, 14 1-5 per cent; at Franklin, 33 per cent.

These statistics prove that the battle of Franklin was the bloodiest of modern times.

Funeral procession, Granbury, Texas, for the man whom the town was named after: Confederate Gen. Hiram B. Granbury. After his death at the Battle of Franklin, Nov. 30, 1864, he was buried in the Polk Cemetery by Ashwood Church near Columbia, Tenn. Twenty-nine years later his remains were transferred to Texas for reinterment, which occurred on November 30, 1893, as shown in the above photo. Granbury's Brigade went into the Battle of Franklin with 650 men. It left with 175.

In concluding the account of this great conflict, I doubt if in any of the bloody battles of the world, from Marathon to Waterloo, from Waterloo to Balaklava, and from Balaklava to Gettysburg, there was more desperate daring than was displayed on some portions of this famous field.

With these facts before us we are better prepared to appreciate the patriotic virtues and splendid manhood of the brave and self-sacrificing officers and men who died here and whose names and deeds we this day commemorate by dedicating to their honor and glory this beautiful and durable monument, erected by the love and gratitude of the noble women of this community, and especially by the Franklin Chapter of the Daughters of the Confederacy, after years of persistent effort and patient perseverance.

And on behalf of every surviving soldier of this battle, and in the name of every sister whose brother and every widow whose husband died on this field, and in behalf of Confederate soldiers everywhere, I want to thank these noble, true, patriotic, and generous Southern women, and all other contributors, who, after so many years of effort, have at last completed this enduring testimonial to the prowess and patriotism, to the valor and virtue of the martyred heroes who perished here. We can never do adequate honor to their names and memories. They died as it became men to die—in defense of the laws, constitution, and independence of their country. Be it said to their glory that they never engaged in a cruel, criminal, and commercial war of aggression, but strictly in a war of defense. We simply withdrew from a voluntary Union of sovereign States in the same solemn, dignified, and peaceable manner in which we entered that Union. This was not done, however, until the terms of that Union had been repeatedly violated and the Constitution of the country and the decision of our highest courts had been denounced and disregarded by the people [that is, Liberals] of the North. The compact of Union had been broken by the [Liberal] Northern States, and the [Conservative] Southern States were no longer bound thereby. So the act of these States in withdrawing therefrom was not an act of treason and rebellion as charged. Besides, the States were sovereign and the units of [autonomous] power. New York, Virginia, and Rhode Island expressly reserved the right, in their acts ratifying the Federal Constitution, to withdraw from the Union whenever the interest and happiness of their people required it. And a reciprocity of principles should surely admit the right of every other State to withdraw whenever the interest and happiness of its people demanded it, especially when there was no provision in the Constitution disallowing the right to secede. Nor was there any provision to coerce a State, should it secede. This was emphatically denied by Hamilton, Livingston, Madison, and others who took a leading part in the formation of the Constitution.[18]

No. We did not want war and we did not inaugurate it. All we asked was to be let alone.[19] But the [Liberal] North, which had become more populous and powerful than the [Conservative] South, determined to preserve her commercial interests, hence the war. If the people of the North had believed that they could have been happier and richer without the South than with her, what rational ground would they then have to expend six billions of money and sacrifice a half million of lives to keep the South in the Union? If the South had been allowed to go in peace, as she desired to do, the North would have lost her richest taxing district—the best patron of her manufacturing and tariff-protected establishments. The South would have opened free trade with Europe, and this would have tended to paralyze, if not pauperize, the great manufacturing industries of the North, and especially of New England. Such a loss was more than they were willing to bear, hence her war of subjugation. Mr. Lincoln disclaimed that the war was to free the slaves, but to save the Union. To save the Union for what purpose? The one I have mentioned—namely, to preserve and augment the commercial interests of the North.[20]

As testified to by Confederate soldiers themselves, those Conservative Southerners who risked their lives at Franklin were not fighting to preserve slavery. They were fighting to preserve the original Constitution (a conservative document) as created by the Founding Fathers—which Liberal Lincoln and the progressive North had promised to overturn.

I have deemed it appropriate to say thus much (though it is little of what could be said) in vindication of the cause for which we fought and our comrades died from the charge of treason and rebellion that we hear and read from day to day. If the charge were not constantly uttered and reiterated, published and republished, I should not have thought it expedient to make any vindication on this solemn and sacred occasion. We were and are no more traitors and rebels than George Washington and his contemporaries. If they had failed, they too would have been called rebels and traitors; but as they succeeded, they have been honored and exalted as heroes and patriots. This is the difference between the accidents of success and failure. And thus we see that the merit of a cause is not to be judged by its success or failure.

Finally, let no man, unchallenged, asperse the memory of our sacred dead, our fallen comrades, with the charge of treason and rebellion. They fell in defense of the liberty and independence of their country, consequently were heroes and patriots. But let their history in granite, so fittingly summarized in the mottoes on this monument, vindicate their memory, pronounce their eulogy, and perpetuate their example. Peace to their spirits! Honor to their ashes![21] — CONFEDERATE GENERAL JOHN BROWN GORDON (delivered at Franklin, Tenn., November 30, 1899)

SEEING THE BATTLE OF FRANKLIN
☛ If all those who claim that their respective commands were at or near the old cotton gin at the battle of Franklin are true, then it is but natural to conclude that the major part of Hood's army was centered at this historic spot. I do not affirm nor contradict these statements, but I am positive that my battery, Douglass's First Texas, was located at this spot, and, although directly on the firing line, took no part in this bloody encounter, from the

very fact that the infantry was in too close proximity for our guns to be used without endangering the lives of our own troops, and it is well to state that this battle was fought by the infantry arm of the service.

If memory serves me correctly, the Seventh Texas and First Tennessee lapped each other across the pike directly in front of us. It has been repeatedly affirmed that the horse of Gen. Cleburne was killed upon the breastworks, when the truth is that he was at least fifty yards from the works when the fatal bullet struck him. If there was a horse killed on the breastworks, it is more than likely it was that of Gen. Adams, who himself fell while leading his men over the enemy's fortifications.

A great blunder was made by some one; for had there not been, then the bloodiest battle of the war, while it lasted, could have been averted by a flank movement [Forrest's idea], thus compelling the enemy to evacuate this stronghold, and in so doing save the lives of some of the grandest heroes that ever fell in battle in defense of a cause that is held as sacred to-day as in 1861-1865.[22] — CONFEDERATE SOLDIER P. E. HOCKERSMITH (Woodburn, Ky.)

GALLANTRY OF A STAFF OFFICER

☛ At the opening of the bloody battle of Franklin, Tenn., there occurred the most thrilling act of bravery I ever witnessed. I belonged to the famous "Whitworth Rifles" detachment of long range sharpshooters of Cheatham's grand old Division. This Division was the front one of Hood's army in the advance from Spring Hill to Franklin. Our position on the march was always in front of the Division, and we were thus the advance of our army.

The Federals were tardy in their retreat when in a few miles of Franklin, but our detachment was commanded by that veteran master of skirmish line tactics, the hard-fighting Lieutenant John M. Ozanne, and, by tactics peculiar to our arm of the service, we manouvered every Federal soldier

"The Federal artillery began firing all along our front, throwing their shells high over our heads at the line of battle."

into their works with but a single shot. We took position on Merrill's hill, a high, rocky, sparsely wooded elevation about twelve hundred yards south of the Carter house, and the line of battle commenced forming back at the Winstead hills, a mile or more to our rear. Soon the Federal artillery began firing all along our front, throwing their shells high over our heads at the line of battle as it formed in our rear. As soon as possible we trained our guns on the Federal gunners, which we could then see through the embrasures in their second line of earthworks. After a while our skirmish line, composed of men about five or six yards apart, in single line, advanced to the attack. Over the ridge they came and down the slope of the hill they went into the level valley below, with step as proud and knightly as though they were princes of the whole earth.

Several hundred yards in advance of the foot of the hill was the first Federal line of earthworks running from the Columbia pike to the west and several hundred yards long. When the skirmish line passed our position on the north apex of the hill, I was forcibly struck with the very peculiar appearance of the officer in command. His eyes teemed strangely brilliant as the fire of battle blazed in them, his ruddy face seemed all aglow with intrepid valor, while a halo of martial glory seemed to surround him as down the slope he went, with horse at full speed, riding as gracefully and as chivalrously as a knight of old.

The Carter House, Franklin, Tenn., area of some of the most desperate and violent fighting.

Soon they had reached a position in easy rifle range of the Federal works, and I supposed the officer would halt and wait till the line of battle came up to reinforce him. He did not do so, but took position in front of the line and at full speed dashed from one end of his line to the other, encouraging his men by his daring and dash.

About this time I became convinced that he was going to charge the line of Federal works with his skirmish line, and although Federal shells and thousands of minie balls from sharpshooters all along their second line of earthworks were whizzing near me, I was so thrilled and entranced that I ceased firing and stood still in order to take in the whole of the impending tragedy. Instead of resisting the onset of the skirmish line, the Federals gave up their works without firing a shot and, seeing his advantage, the intrepid commander pressed his skirmish line forward in quick time and gained on the Federals, so that about the time the last of them scaled their works, the skirmish line got into the ditch in front. This saved the skirmish line from a withering fire which would have been given them but for the retreating Federals.

This officer was Major Joseph Vaulx, now of Nashville, who was on Major-General Frank Cheatham's staff. This is written without his knowledge or consent, as I have not met him since the war, but I desire that your thousands of readers may know who led that gallant and brilliant advance in the face of almost certain annihilation. Long may Major Vaulx live to wear in peace the knightly wreath he that day so gallantly snatched from the gory brow of grim-visaged war.[23] — CONFEDERATE SOLDIER I. N. SHANNON (Goodlettsville, Tenn.)

GEN. JOHN ADAMS AT FRANKLIN

☛ [Concerning Confederate] Gen. Adams's tragic death at Franklin . . . He survived only a few minutes, his horse being killed instantly while astride the works, making it one of the most striking pictures of heroism ever seen. The brigade entered the fight about four o'clock from the rear and east of Col. John H. McGavock's house Carnton Plantation].[24] Gen. Adams was about ten paces in front of his line of battle, and thus led his troops for about half a mile. Capt. Thomas Gibson, his cousin and a member of his staff, says that he was calm and self-possessed, vigilantly watching and directing the movements of his men. When about fifty yards from the enemy's works he rode rapidly from near the right of his brigade to near the left, then directed his course toward the enemy, and fell on their works pierced with nine

Gen. John Adams' horse sitting dead atop the works, with his Confederate owner lying dead nearby.

bullets. He was wounded severely in his right arm near the shoulder early in the fight, and was urged to leave the field, but said: "No; I am going to see my men through." The brigade suffered terribly, having over four hundred and fifty killed and wounded, many field and line officers being of the number.[25] — CONFEDERATE SARGENT-MAJOR SUMNER A. CUNNINGHAM

"THE MOST GALLANT ACTION OF THE WAR"

☛ I accompanied Gen. Frank Cheatham to Louisville, Ky., when his paper on the affair at Spring Hill was read before the Confederate Historical Society of that city. There were present many soldiers of the Federal and Confederate armies, and the paper referred to naturally brought up the Franklin campaign and the disastrous battle at the town of Franklin. A superb banquet followed the society meeting, and after that a dozen or more gentlemen gathered around Gen. Cheatham and myself, and Hood's unfortunate campaign was fought over again.

Finally a gentleman, whose name I cannot now recall, who commanded a Federal regiment at the point assailed by Adams's Brigade, addressing myself, said: "Tell us something of the personal history of Gen. John Adams."

I gave him a general outline of his career. He then added: "His conduct at Franklin was the grandest performance of the war. I watched him as he led his brigade against our works. He looked like a soldier inspired with the belief that the fortunes of his cause depended upon his own actions; and when his horse leaped upon our works for one moment there was a cessation of firing, caused, no doubt, by admiration of his lofty courage. Another moment, as he called to his command to follow, a volley was delivered and rider and horse fell dead inside of our works."

John Adams, C.S.A.

The Hon. James Speed, of Kentucky, was present, and was an interested listener. He had been a cabinet officer of Mr. Lincoln's. He said: "Colonel, why did you kill so brave a man? Why not have caused his capture?"

The Colonel replied: "If we had paused to demand his surrender, he would have crossed the works and cut our line and held it." He added, addressing Gen. Cheatham: "If Gen. Adams had made the attack on your extreme left, he would have carried the works, and Nashville would have been yours without a battle."

Maj. Sanders, of the Confederate army, Capt. Speed, of the Federal army, and many others now living were present, with some familiarity with the conduct of the officers and men of the Army of Tennessee. I have long been of the opinion that the conduct of Gen. John Adams at the battle of Franklin was the most gallant action of the war.[26] — CONFEDERATE OFFICER JAMES DAVIS PORTER (on the staff of Gen. Benjamin F. Cheatham)

"THE DEATH-ANGEL GATHERS ITS LAST HARVEST"

☛ Kind reader, right here my pen, and courage, and ability fail me. I shrink from butchery. Would to God I could tear the page from these memoirs and from my own memory. It is the blackest page in the history of the war of the Lost Cause.[27] It was the bloodiest battle of modern times in any war. It was the finishing stroke to the independence of the Southern Confederacy. I was there. I saw it. My flesh trembles, and creeps, and crawls when I think of it to-day. My heart almost ceases to beat at the horrid recollection. Would to God that I had never witnessed such a scene!

I cannot describe it. It beggars description. I will not attempt to describe it. I could not. The death-angel was there to gather its last harvest. It was the grand coronation of death. Would that I could turn the page. But

I feel, though I did so, that page would still be there, teeming with its scenes of horror and blood. I can only tell of what I saw.

Our regiment was resting in the gap of a range of hills in plain view of the city of Franklin. We could see the battle flags of the enemy waving in the breeze. Our army had been depleted of its strength by a forced march from Spring Hill, and stragglers lined the road. Our artillery had not yet come up, and could not be brought into action. Our cavalry was across [the] Harpeth river, and our army was but in poor condition to make an assault. While resting on this hill-side, I saw a courier dash up to our commanding general, B. F. Cheatham, and the word, "Attention!" was given. I knew then that we would soon be in action. Forward, march. We passed over the hill and through a little skirt of woods.

The enemy were fortified right across the Franklin pike, in the suburbs of the town. Right here in these woods a detail of skirmishers was called for. Our regiment was detailed. We deployed as skirmishers, firing as we advanced on the left of the turnpike road. If I had not been a skirmisher on that day, I would not have been writing this to-day, in the year of our Lord 1882.

It was four o'clock on that dark and dismal December day when the line of battle was formed, and those devoted heroes were ordered forward, to "strike for their altars and their fires, for the green graves of their sires, for God and their native land."

"Johnny Reb," the typical Confederate soldier (shown here), was traditional, conservative, Christian, and pro-constitution.

As they marched on down through an open field toward the rampart of blood and death, the Federal batteries began to open and mow down and gather into the garner of death, as brave and good, and pure spirits as the world ever saw. The twilight of evening had begun to gather as a precursor of the coming blackness of midnight darkness that was to envelop a scene so sickening and horrible that it is impossible for me to describe it. "Forward, men," is repeated all along the line. A sheet of fire was poured into our very faces, and for a moment we halted as if in despair, as the terrible avalanche of shot and shell laid low those brave and gallant heroes, whose bleeding wounds attested that the struggle would be desperate. Forward, men! The air loaded with death-dealing missiles. Never on this earth did men fight against such terrible odds. It seemed that the very elements of heaven and earth were in one mighty uproar. Forward, men! And the blood spurts in a perfect jet from the dead and wounded. The earth is red with blood. It runs in streams, making little rivulets as it flows. Occasionally there was a little lull in the storm of battle, as the men were loading their guns, and for a few moments it seemed as if night tried to cover the scene with her mantle. The death-angel shrieks and laughs and old Father Time is busy with his sickle, as he gathers in the last harvest of death, crying, "More, more, more!" while his rapacious maw is glutted with the slain.

But the [Confederate] skirmish line being deployed out, extending a little wider than the battle did—passing through a thicket of small locusts, where Brown, orderly sergeant of Company B, was killed—we advanced on toward the breastworks, on and on. I had made up my mind to die—felt glorious.

We pressed forward until I heard the terrific roar of battle open on our right. Cleburne's division was charging their works. I passed on until I got to their works, and got over on their [the Yankees'] side. But in fifty yards of where I was the scene was lit up by fires that seemed like hell itself. It appeared to be but one line of streaming fire. Our troops were upon one side of the breastworks, and the Federals on the other. I ran up on the line of works, where our men were engaged. Dead soldiers filled the entrenchments. The firing was kept up until after midnight, and gradually died out.

"The earth was red with blood. . . the scene was lit up by fires that seemed like hell itself."

We passed the night where we were. But when the morrow's sun began to light up the eastern sky with its rosy hues, and we looked over the battlefield, O, my God! what did we see! It was a grand holocaust of death. Death had held high carnival there that night. The dead were piled the one on the other all over the ground. I never was so horrified and appalled in my life. Horses, like men, had died game on the gory breastworks. General Adams' horse had his fore feet on one side of the works and his hind feet on the other, dead. The general seems to have been caught so that he was held to the horse's back, sitting almost as if living, riddled, and mangled, and torn with balls. General Cleburne's mare had her fore feet on top of the works, dead in that position. General Cleburne's body was pierced with forty-nine bullets, through and through. General Strahl's horse lay by the roadside and the general by his side, both dead, and all his staff. General Gist, a noble and brave cavalier from South Carolina, was lying with his sword reaching across the breastworks still grasped in his hand. He was lying there dead. All dead!

They sleep in the graveyard yonder at Ashwood, almost in sight of my home, where I am writing to-day. They sleep the sleep of the brave. We love and cherish their memory. They sleep beneath the ivy-mantled walls of St. John's church, where they expressed a wish to be buried. The private soldier sleeps where he fell, piled in one mighty heap. Four thousand five hundred privates! all lying side by side in death! Thirteen generals were killed and wounded. Four thousand five hundred men slain, all piled and heaped together at one place. I cannot tell the number of others killed and wounded. God alone knows that. We'll all find out on the morning of the final resurrection.

Kind friends, I have attempted in my poor and feeble way to tell you of this (I can hardly call it) battle. It should be called by some other name. But, like all other battles, it, too, has gone into history. I leave it with you. I do not know who was to blame. It lives in the memory of the poor old Rebel soldier who went through that trying and terrible ordeal.

We shed a tear for the dead. They are buried and forgotten. We meet no more on earth. But up yonder, beyond the sunset and the night, away beyond the clouds and tempest, away beyond the stars that ever twinkle and shine in the blue vault above us, away yonder by the great white throne, and by the river of life, where the Almighty and Eternal God sits, surrounded by the angels and archangels and the redeemed of earth, we will meet again and see those noble and brave spirits who gave up their lives for their country's cause [conservatism] that night at Franklin, Tennessee.

A life given for one's country is never lost. It blooms again beyond the grave in a land of beauty and of love. Hanging around the throne of sapphire and gold, a rich garland awaits the

The grave site of Sam Watkins, Zion Presbyterian Church Cemetery, Mt. Pleasant, Tenn. (Photo Lochlainn Seabrook)

coming of him who died for his country, and when the horologe of time has struck its last note upon his dying brow, Justice hands the record of life to Mercy, and Mercy pleads with Jesus, and God, for his sake, receives him in his eternal home beyond the skies at last and forever.[28] — CONFEDERATE PRIVATE SAMUEL RUSH "SAM" WATKINS (Company H, 1st Tennessee Regiment)

SOLDIERING WITH GEN. STRAHL IN "THE VALLEY OF DEATH"

☞ This sketch of the battle of Franklin, though not intended as an especial tribute to Gen. Strahl, is published in this connection with no greater desire than to honor the memory of that gallant soldier and devout Christian. The removal [by President Jefferson Davis] of Gen. [Joseph E.] Johnston and the appointment of Hood to succeed him in command of the Army of Tennessee, was an astounding event. So devoted to Johnston were his men that the presence and immediate command of Gen. [Robert E.] Lee would not have been accepted without complaint. They were so satisfied that even in retreat they did not lose their faith in ultimate success. They were not reconciled to the change until the day before the battle of Franklin. The successful crossing of Duck River that morning [November 29, 1864] at an early hour, and the march to Spring Hill, where the Federal retreat was so nearly cut off (a failure for which it was understood Gen. Hood was not to blame), created an enthusiasm for him equal to that entertained for Stonewall Jackson after his extraordinary achievements. That night the extensive valley east of Spring Hill was lighted up by our thousands of camp fires, in plain view of, and close proximity to, the retreating lines of the enemy.

A 1904 view from the top of Winstead Hill looking north to Franklin. The Columbia Pike cuts through the middle of the area from left to right. Gen. Hood would have witnessed a similar scene on the morning of November 30, 1864.

The next morning [November 30, 1864], as we marched in quick time toward Franklin, we were confirmed in our impressions of Federal alarm. I counted on the way thirty-four wagons that had been abandoned on the smooth turnpike. In some instances whole teams of mules had been killed to prevent their capture. A few miles south of Franklin the Federal lines of infantry were deployed, and our progress was checked; but we pressed them without delay until they retired behind the outer works about the town. Soon after they withdrew from the range of hills south, overlooking the place, and we were advanced to its crest. I happened, though in the line of battle (as I was "right guide" to my regiment), to be close to where Gen. Hood halted his staff and rode alone to the top of the hill [Winstead], and with his field glasses surveyed the situation. It was an extraordinary moment. Those of us who were near could see, as private soldiers rarely did, the position of both armies. Although Franklin was some two miles in the distance, the plain presented a scene of great commotion. But I was absorbed in the one man whose mind was deciding the fate of thousands. With an arm and a leg in the grave, and with the consciousness that he had not until within a couple of days won the confidence which his army had in his predecessor, he had now a very trying ordeal to pass through. It was all-important to act, if at all, at once. He rode to Stephen D. Lee, the nearest of his subordinate generals, and, shaking hands with him cordially, announced his decision to make an immediate charge.

William W. Loring, C.S.A.

No event of the war perhaps showed a scene equal to this. The range of hills upon which we formed offered the best view of the battlefield, with but little exposure to danger, and there were hundreds collected there as spectators. Our ranks were being extended rapidly to the right and left. In Franklin there was the utmost confusion. The enemy was greatly excited. We could see them running to and fro. Wagon-trains were being pressed across the Harpeth river, and on toward Nashville. Gen. [William W.] Loring, of Cleburne's division, made a speech to his men. Our Brigadier-General Strahl was quiet, and there was an expression of sadness on his face. The soldiers were full of ardor, and confident of success. They had unbounded faith in Gen. Hood, whom they believed would achieve a victory that would give us Nashville. Such was the spirit of the army as the signal was given which set it in motion.

Our generals were ready, and some of them rode in front of our main line. With a quickstep, we moved forward to the sound of stirring music. This is the only battle that I was in, and they were many, where bands of music were used. I was right guide to the Forty-first Tennessee, marching four paces to the front I had an opportunity of viewing my comrades, and well remember the look of determination that was on every face. Our bold movement caused the enemy to give up, without much firing, its advanced line. As they fell back at double-quick, our men rushed forward, even though they had to face the grim line of breastworks just at the edge of the town.

Before we were in proper distance for small arms, the artillery opened on both sides. Our guns, firing over our heads from the hills in the rear, used ammunition without stint, while the enemy's batteries were at constant play upon our lines. When they withdrew to their main line of works, it was as one even plain for a mile. About fifty yards in front of their breastworks, we came in contact with formidable *chevaux de frise*, over or through which it was very difficult to pass. Why half of us were not killed, yet remains a mystery; for after moving forward so great a distance, all the time under fire, the detention, immediately in their front, gave them a very great advantage. We arrived at the works, and some of our men after a club fight at the trenches, got over. The colors [flag] of my regiment were carried inside, and when the arm that held them was shot off, they fell to the ground and remained until morning. Cleburne's men dashed at the works, but their gallant leader was shot dead, and they gave way, so that the enemy remained on our flank, and kept up constant enfilading fire.

Our left also failed to hold the works, and for a short distance we remained and fought until the ditch was almost full of dead men. Night came on soon after the hard fighting began, and we fired at the flash of each other's guns. Holding the enemy's lines, as we continued to do on this part of them, we were terribly massacred by the enfilade firing. The works were so high that those who fired the guns were obliged to get a footing in the embankment, exposing themselves in addition to their flank, to a fire by men in houses. One especially severe was that from Mr. Carter's, immediately in my front. I was near Gen. Strahl, who stood in the ditch, and handed up guns to those posted to fire them. I had passed to him my short Enfield (noted in the regiment) about the sixth time. The man who had been firing cocked it and was taking deliberate aim, when he was shot and tumbled down dead into the ditch upon those killed before him. When the men so exposed were shot down, their places were supplied by volunteers until these were exhausted, and it was necessary for

Otho F. Strahl, C.S.A.

Gen. Strahl to call upon others. He turned to me, and though I was several feet back from the ditch, I rose up immediately, and walking over the wounded and dead, took position with one foot upon the pile of bodies of my dead fellows, and the other in the embankment, and fired guns which the General himself handed up to me until he, too, was shot down. One other man had had position on my right, and assisted in the firing.

The battle lasted until not an efficient man was left between us and the Columbia Pike, about fifty yards to our right, and hardly enough behind us to hand up the guns. We could not hold out much longer, for indeed, but

few of us were then left alive. It seemed as if we had no choice but to
surrender or try to get away, and when I asked the General for counsel, he
simply answered, "Keep firing." But just as the man to my right was shot,
and fell against me with terrible groans, Gen. Strahl was shot. He threw up
his hands, falling on his face, and I thought him dead, but in asking the dying
man, who still lay against my shoulder as he sank forever, how he was
wounded, the General, who had not been killed, thinking my question was
to him, raised up saying that he was shot in the neck, and called for Col.
Stafford to turn over his command.

He crawled over the dead, the ditch being three deep, about twenty feet
to where Col. Stafford was. His staff officers started to carry him to the
rear, but he received another shot, and directly the third, which killed him
instantly. Col. Stafford was dead in the pile, as the morning light disclosed,

with his feet wedged in at the bottom, with
other dead across and under him after he fell,
leaving his body half standing as if ready to
give command to the dead! By that time but
a handful of us were left on that part of the
line, and as I was sure that our condition was
not known, I ran to the rear to report to Gen.
John C. Brown, commanding the division. I
met Major Hampton of his staff, who told me
that Gen. Brown was wounded, and that Gen.
Strahl was in command. This assured me that
those in command did not know the real
situation, so I went on the hunt for General
Cheatham. By and by relief was sent to the
front. This done, nature gave way. My
shoulder was black with bruises from firing,

Sumner A. Cunningham, C.S.A.

and it seemed that no moisture was left in my system. Utterly exhausted,
I sank upon the ground and tried to sleep.

The battle was over, and I could do no more; but animated still with
concern for the fate of comrades, I returned to the awful spectacle in search
of some who year after year had been at my side. Ah the loyalty of faithful
comrades in such a struggle!

These personal recollections are all that I can give as the greater part of
the battle was fought after nightfall, and once in the midst of it, with but the
light of the flashing guns, I could see only what passed directly under my
own eyes. True, the moon was shining; but the dense smoke and dust so
filled the air as to weaken its benefits, like a heavy fog before the rising sun,
only there was no promise of the fog disappearing. Our spirits were
crushed. It was indeed the Valley of Death.[29] — CONFEDERATE
SARGENT-MAJOR SUMNER A. CUNNINGHAM

VIVID REMINISCENCES OF FRANKLIN

☛ I participated in the battle of Franklin as a private [boy] soldier in the Twenty-fourth Tennessee, the right regiment of Gen. Strahl's Brigade. Gen. French is correct as to Loring commanding the right division of Stewart's Corps, and being on the extreme right of the line during the engagement. It was Gen. [Mark P.] Lowrey, of Cleburne's Division, whom you heard make a speech to his brigade.

. . . Cleburne's left dressed on the right, and Brown's right on the left of the pike. Gen. Edward Johnson's Division of Lee's Corps marched just in rear of Cheatham's Corps, and if Lee was at the head of his command [S. A. Cunningham was] . . . doubtless correct as to Gen. Hood addressing Gen. Lee. It is true Lee was at Columbia the day before, but the head of his command was at Rutherford Creek the next morning, only six miles south of Spring Hill, and Lee himself could have been on the ground. The two Mississippi brigades of Edward Johnson's Division, Lee's Corps, made a gallant and heroic charge on the left of Brown's line between sundown and dark, and were repulsed with heavy loss, as was manifested by the numbers of their dead left on the ground. There was but one Confederate battery engaged until after dark. It was Bledsoe's, from Missouri, which moved down the pike with Strahl's Brigade. After losing their horses they pushed their guns [cannon] forward by hand. The Federal line of battle on their right, and Confederate left of the Columbia pike, was much longer than on their left, or Confederate right of said pike, which was the cause of so much lapping of the Southern troops on the right, and why so many troops of different divisions assailed the enemy at and around the old gin-house.

The pike being Cleburne's left guide, as he advanced his division obliquely to the right, lapping the corps of Gens. Stuart, Cleburne, Walthall, and French. These divisions all assailed the works at that point. To the credit of Brown's Tennessee Division, with Gist's Brigade of South Carolina and Georgia troops, be it said, they

Edward C. Walthall, C.S.A.

assailed the Federal works without lapping, and drove the enemy from their main line of ditches. The two right brigades of his division, Gordon's and Strahl's, although heavily pressed from both flanks from an enfilading fire, never once yielded the advantage gained. The Federal troops were withdrawn from their extreme right and placed in front of these two brigades. On that part of the line the heavy night fighting was done. While the greater number of the Confederate dead lay in front and near the gin-house, the Federal dead were thickest around the Carter house in front of these two brigades. Strahl's Brigade was composed of the Nineteenth, Twenty-fourth, and Forty-first consolidated Tennessee regiments. Lieut. Col. S. E. Shannon, of the Twenty-fourth, was severely wounded in the neck from the top of the Federal works.

Imagine the dangerous position of those troops while fighting large odds in front with great masses of the enemy on their right side in the same line of works! These men held their position without flinching until the enemy were all gone. I myself lay so close to a Federal battery that every time it fired I could feel the heat. I remember having seen Gen. Strahl in the works when we first reached them. He was assisting one of the Nineteenth Tennessee in climbing over. Those who went over had to be helped. The works were much higher on this part of the line than on the right and around the gin-house. He afterward moved to the left, and I saw him no more. This will answer [the question] . . . as to the point of the high works.

. . . I endeavored, just a year ago. to mark the positions held by the various [Confederate] troops, and line of Federal ditches in this battle, and the points where the various Generals were killed, and stationed posts to designate these places. . . .[30] — CONFEDERATE PRIVATE B. T. ROBERTS (Franklin Tenn.)

BATTLE OF FRANKLIN RECALLED

☛ I witnessed an example of nerve at the battle of Franklin which takes rank with the most notable of thousands during the war. Gen. Thomas M. Scott, of Louisiana, the adjutant-general of his brigade, the writer, and several other wounded officers of the stall and line, were quartered at the McGavock home [Carnton Plantation] after the battle.[31] I recall the agony of Col. W. S. Nelson, of the Twelfth Louisiana, as he lay dying, torn to pieces by a discharge of grape and canister at close range. "My poor wife and child! my poor wife and child! Can you not get the surgeons to administer some drug that will relieve me of this torture?" I did try, though my appeals were in vain. I could imagine what he suffered as the cold perspiration gathered in knots on his brow, and, of course, knew that death was inevitable.

Carnton Plantation (rear view), Franklin, Tenn., as it looked in the late 19th Century.

The case of immediate reference here, however, was that of a [Confederate] Capt. [Roland W.] Jones, from Grenada, Miss. He was lying on the floor. One of his thighs had been shattered by a cannon-ball; the bone of the other had been laid bare by a like discharge. One of his arms was also shattered and, as I recall it, one of his hands had been torn away. He was the worst wounded man I ever saw, except that no vital organs had been lacerated, as in the case of Col. Nelson and others.

At Capt. Jones's side knelt Dr. George C. Phillips, of Lexington, Miss., the manly surgeon of the Twenty-Second Mississippi, ministering to his wounds. "Captain, it would subject you to useless pain to amputate your leg," said the tender-hearted young surgeon. "The wound is fatal, or would be by amputation." "You are right, Doctor," replied Capt. Jones; "but I don't intend to have that leg cut off, and I don't intend to die. I want to hold on to what is left of me. Why, bless your soul!" he added, holding up his shattered hand, as a smile passed over his face, "there is enough left of me to make a first-class cavalryman."

This was said in reference to the old joke which infantry soldiers good-naturedly were used to getting off on the brave riders of the Confederacy.

I do not know what finally became of Capt. Jones. I have heard that his fractured leg grew together after a fashion, and that he was living several years ago.[32] — CONFEDERATE SOLDIER C. E. MERRILL

"I WILL SHOOT THE FIRST MAN WHO PUTS A KNIFE IN IT"

☛ The reference made by C. E. Merrill [in the previous entry] . . . to the nerve exhibited by Capt. Roland W. Jones, who was so desperately wounded at the battle of Franklin, awakens memories of the past. The incident is well remembered by Col. M. D. L. Stephens, of this place, who commanded the Thirty-first Mississippi Regiment, and who was also badly wounded, and was with Capt. Jones and others in the McGavock House [Carnton Plantation] at the time.[33]

Capt. Jones was from this county (Yalobusha), and commanded a company in Rayburn's Battalion. He not only saved enough of himself "to make a cavalryman," but he also lived to serve his country in civil life with equal honors as those won upon the bloody field at Franklin. He married one of the ladies who waited on him while wounded, and the children of that union are now of the first people of this state. Capt. Jones never fully recovered from his wounds, and died about four years ago, the soul of honor and loved by all who knew him.

Col. Stephens had good cause to remember the conversation that occurred, for, after turning from Capt. Jones, the surgeon said to him: "Well, Colonel, we will certainly have to amputate your leg." Col. Stephens himself was too weak to refuse, but there was a Dr. Wall present, who had promised the Colonel not to allow his limb taken off, and he protested; and when the surgeon seemed determined he said: "I promised Col. Stephens I would not allow his leg taken off, and I will shoot the first man who puts a knife on it." The surgeon remarked, "Well, there is no use being a fool about it!" and walked off.

Col. Stephens recovered, and is to-day in full enjoyment of health and limbs. He is Commander of Featherston Camp No. 517, United Confederate Veterans.[34] — J. T. BLOUNT (Water Valley, Miss.)

THE BATTLE OF FRANKLIN

☞ I belonged to Company H, Third Mississippi regiment, Lowrey's brigade, Cleburne's division. The regiment was raised by Gen. Lowrey, and when he was promoted to brigadier it was commanded by Col. H. H. Tyson. He was in command at Franklin. Our company, E and H consolidated, was commanded by Capt. W. W. Nance, a brave soldier still living near Ripley, Miss.

Our entire command realized beforehand that the battle of Franklin would be a bloody affair. We saw their formidable works surmounted by artillery and supported by strong lines of infantry. About 3 P.M. the advance was ordered. I distinctly recall seeing Gen. Pat Cleburne on going into the charge with us. He was mounted on a large light bay horse; was dressed in full uniform, and wore the magnificent sword presented him by his old regiment, the First Arkansas. No knightlier soul ever lived than Gen. Cleburne.

As we swept forward the fire of the enemy's skirmishers became hot, but we brushed them from their outside line of rifle pits and pressed onward. When we had crossed over this first line of real breastworks there began that deadly hail of lead and iron which made Franklin's field a scene of unparalleled carnage. Men fell at almost every

Mark P. Lowrey, C.S.A.

step, but onward we pressed across line after line, until our ranks were sadly decimated and we were forced to halt. It was here that the brave Gen. Cleburne fell. He was about sixty yards from me when he was killed, being riddled by a volley. He had in one hand his sword, and in the other a pistol.

Our line stopped against the line of works until daylight, when it was found the enemy had fallen back. Our loss was frightful. Of our company, only two men were uninjured, and these were myself and T. G. Paden, who is now my neighbor and family physician.

I cannot close this sketch without paying a tribute to Gen. Lowrey. He

was a Baptist preacher of singular earnestness and power, and no braver man ever followed the flag of the Confederacy. After the bloody battle of Chickamauga, in which he bore a distinguished part, he was presented to Gen. Bragg by Gen. Hardee with these words: "Gen. Bragg, here is the bravest man in the Confederate army." He never forgot that he was called to preach the gospel, and during seasons of rest from active campaigning would preach to his command with zeal and power. [35] — CONFEDERATE SOLDIER J. C. DEAN (Burnt Mills, Miss.)

William A. Quarles, C.S.A.

MY MEMORIES OF FRANKLIN

☞ Thirty-six years ago I was a humble participant in the battle of Franklin, which I believe was as bloody a contest as ever occurred in the history of the world. I shall not attempt to describe the battle, which has already been done by Gen. Gordon and others. . . .

The circumstances leading up to the battle were highly interesting and dramatic. The command of Gen. Hood reached Columbia, Tenn., November 28 [1864], where we found the enemy intrenched. A picket line was immediately established, and advanced to within view of their works. At daylight on the 29th the pickets were ordered forward, when we found the earthworks abandoned. The enemy had retired across the [Duck] river during the night.

Our regiment, which had been on picket and which had advanced into the town of Columbia, was recalled. Stewart's and Cheatham's corps were ordered to cross the river, about four miles above the town, and proceed without delay to Spring Hill [where a battle was fought that day]. The crossing was effected by a pontoon bridge. The line of march was begun over country roads, and vigorously pursued until about 2 P.M., when we reached the neighborhood of the pike, just in the rear of Spring Hill, where we bivouacked until daylight. We could hear the cannonading at Columbia, which assured us that we had gained our purpose, and had the enemy cut off from relief or escape. Up to this time the management was perfect. If we had formed line of battle across the pike, not a [Union] man could have escaped. The halt was an unfortunate, an inexcusable mistake.

By daylight, when we resumed our march, the enemy retreated along the pike, and had entirely escaped the trap in which they were caught. As we reached the pike the enemy's rear could be discovered on long stretches of road two miles ahead. Gen. Forrest rode by the side of the line, and, overtaking Gen. Quarles, our brigadier, he vigorously condemned him for the display of incapacity. It had a very demoralizing effect on the men. I could hear remarks to the effect that Hood had purposely let them escape in order to gain greater glory from whipping them in their breastworks. There was absolutely no expectation that they could withstand us, as our force was believed to be three to one.

At the Battle of Spring Hill, November 29, 1864, Hood and his men bewilderingly permitted thousands of Union soldiers to march past them in the dead of night, subsequently setting the stage for the Confederate disasters at Franklin and Nashville. This Southern debacle quickly became known as the great "lost opportunity," a topic still being debated to this day.

We pressed them rapidly, marching in quick time. Every one or two hundred yards we would pass an abandoned wagon with the team shot down in the traces. There was every evidence of haste and fright. Our regiment, the First Alabama, headed the column, and on reaching a point from which Franklin could be seen, Gen. Hood raised his lorgnette and gazed intently. As we reached him he gave the command, "By file right," and the march was continued through woods and fields until we reached Harpeth River, back of Franklin. On reaching this point we were halted and formed line of battle. The manner of our approach to the town placed the right much nearer Franklin than the left, and the execution of a right wheel was necessary to adjust the trouble.

We were now within a half mile of Franklin, and ready for the advance. I could see the line for a half mile on each side, and it was grand. The generals and colonels were all ahead of the line, and from appearances were perfectly indifferent to the danger of the situation. The command forward was given. The line stepped off promptly, while a band or two on a near elevation began to play "Dixie," which elicited a Rebel yell that doubtless struck terror into the hearts of the Federals crouching behind their imposing breastworks. There were two lines of works in our front, and, as we advanced, the enemy precipitately withdrew to the second. Though the firing was pretty heavy, very little damage was done.

When we reached the first line of breastworks, the men seemed to think the trouble was over, and fell down to avoid the bullets. The command "Forward!" was again given, but the men did not go. I climbed on top of the breastworks and repeated the command several times without effect, and, seeing the line on my right going forward, I hastened to attach myself to it.

On reaching the second line of works, in which the Federals were standing and firing with all the rapidity possible, I fell down behind it and ceased to be an actor in the great tragedy of war. For an hour I witnessed as sublime bursts of courage as it is possible for human beings to display. The gallantry of [Frederick] Hobson, which startled the world by its dramatic splendor, is a mere trifle when compared with the unspeakably desperate courage which characterized the attack and defense of Franklin. For more than an hour two lines of men fought with but a pile of dirt between them. In firing, the muzzles of the guns would pass each other, and nine times out of ten, when a man rose to fire, he fell back dead.

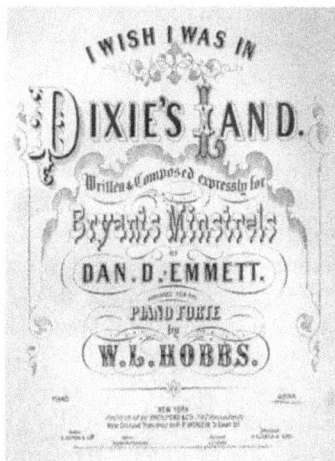

A Southern favorite, "Dixie" was one of the songs played at the Battle of Franklin—to an accompanying enthusiastic chorus of Rebel yells.

It is to be remembered that the troops were all in confusion, that there were no organized commands. Officers and soldiers had straggled forward to this point of certain and swift death, and they determined to kill as many as possible in the few minutes they had to live. At frequent intervals the men would rise with the determination to go over and fight it out. Three times Col. Dick Williams rose with the cry, "Follow me!" and three times I seized the tail of his coat and held him back.

A student of history, commenting upon the battle, writes this opinion: "No man was sanguine enough to feel that he could reach the second line and live, and yet there were many who dared to approach it. The history of the world may record parallel cases, but there will never be found a page of more surpassing heroic splendors than the one that tells of the men in gray at the battle of Franklin."[36] — CONFEDERATE SOLDIER D. H. PATTERSON (Arcadia, La.)

WHY THE SOUTH WAS THE REAL VICTOR AT FRANKLIN

☛ . . . The Louisiana Brigade was among the troops left at Columbia, while others proceeded to Spring Hill. . . . The next day we received orders to move at once toward Franklin, and I remember well of a halt being made, and that the good news was made known to the troops that we had the enemy between the upper and nether millstones, and for us to hurry up or we would not be in it.

We increased our steps, but we learned on our approach to Franklin that the enemy had got from between the millstones and were safe behind their works, and the battle was on. My regiment was held in reserve. I stood close by Gen. S. D. Lee and Gen. Frank Cheatham, and in that way I saw the battle from first to its close.

Hiram B. Granbury, C.S.A.

After dark we could tell how our troops were gaining by the line of fire from their guns. During the battle S. D. Lee [said]: "Gen. Granbury says for God's sake send more men." I heard one of Gen. Granbury's aids report to Gen. Lee: "Send him some troops. He is now behind the last line of the enemy's works, but out of ammunition, and the trenches are running in blood." Soon after Gen. Granbury was numbered with the dead.[37]

This fight could have been averted. . . . It was common talk that if the troops had been thrown across the pike the Federal army would not have reached Franklin as they did. In a conversation afterwards with Gen. Randall L. Gibson, commanding the Louisiana Brigade, he said to me: "The whole thing is inexplicable. Some one blundered, and the bloodiest and most disastrous battle of the war was fought and won by the bravery and self-sacrifice of the Confederate soldiers."[38] — CONFEDERATE COLONEL R. H. LINDSAY (16th Louisiana Regiment)

IN PRAISE OF THE ARMY OF TENNESSEE

☛ . . . The men of the West recognize the desperate valor and the inexhaustible courage which distinguished this great struggle [the Battle of Antietam]. They have only to speak in praise and commendation of all that was done by their comrades of the East on that fearful occasion; but away in the West, on the bloody field of Franklin, there was a more than counterpart of the destruction and horrors of Antietam. In the battle of Franklin it was reserved for the Army of Tennessee to make its last great struggle, and in that struggle to suffer practical annihilation, but in its death to leave a monument of noble manhood and patriotic courage which will stand coterminous with time itself.

Sherman had gone upon his march to the sea; Hood had commenced his campaign through Tennessee and Alabama, and had reached Franklin, Tenn., on the 30th of November, 1864, where he formed his 20,000 men to assault the Federal soldiers under Gen. Schofield. This small remnant of those hosts who so earnestly and so gallantly had defended Tennessee, Kentucky, Alabama, Mississippi, and Georgia for three years past alone remained.

As the Confederate army on the ridge looked down and across the valley at the other side, some two miles away, where the Federals were intrenched, these 20,000 undismayed and gallant patriots presented one of the most imposing and

Arthur M. Manigault, C.S.A.

thrilling scenes that had marked the conduct of the great war. One of the assaulting columns was led by the impetuous and chivalrous Cleburne. No troops ever passed through more tremendous discharges of artillery and small arms than these men from Tennessee, Mississippi, Missouri, Arkansas, Louisiana, Alabama, South Carolina, North Carolina, and Kentucky on that terrible day. By their valor they found a resting place in part behind the works of their enemies, but it was only the rest of death.

Of the Confederates engaged in this conflict, the loss reached the enormous figures of thirty-three percent. Pickett, in his world-renowned charge, lost twenty-one per cent, while the infantry engaged at Franklin lost thirty-three per cent. Thirteen regimental commanders were killed, thirty-two wounded, and nine captured. Of the four brigadier generals in Brown's Division, Carter, Gist, and Strahl were killed and Gordon captured, and the major general was so severely wounded that his division was commanded by a colonel the next day. Maj. Gen. Cleburne, Gen. Granbury, and Gen. John Adams lay dead; while Gen. Cockrell, Gen. Manigault, Gen. Quarles, and Gen. Scott were wounded. In proportion to the number of men engaged, the battle of Franklin was the bloodiest of modern times, and in proportion to the number of officers who entered this conflict no other battle presents more terrible losses. For daring and desperate courage and mortality the battle of Franklin stands out as one of the most memorable conflicts of any war.

Time fails for the details of this awful and wonderful battle. The men of the West answer back to the men of the East that, whatever may have occurred at Antietam, worse occurred at Franklin, and the conduct and the courage of these Southern and Southwestern men at Franklin entitle them to a full share in the enduring record of that immortality which Confederate soldiers purchased with their life blood.

The Army of Tennessee had been called upon during its entire existence to endure peculiar and unusual privations, and to meet extraordinary reverses. The topographical conditions, its wide separations from the Confederate capital, its liability to be flanked by forces transported along thousands of miles of navigable streams render its location uncertain, and after all its defeats it was a sad fate in a last noble response to the call of duty to meet practical annihilation. . . .[39] — CONFEDERATE COL. BENNETT H. YOUNG (from an address at a UCV Reunion at Memphis, Tenn.)

MEMORIES OF GENERAL JOHN ADAMS

☞ Gen. John Adams was a kingly man without the royalty usually attached to that class. He was a true type of the American, or rather Southern, soldier—ever modest, conservative, brave, and patriotic. He seemed not to know fear. To do his duty at all times and under all circumstances was ever his desire.

No truer or braver officer ever gave his life in defense of his beloved Southland. The last words I heard of his saying was in that terrible and ever-memorable charge on the Federal works at Franklin. Riding in front of his brigade, he turned his face to his men and said in a cool, calm, deliberate tone: "Follow me, my men!" In almost less time than it takes me to write, his horse sank down with his front feet resting on the enemy's breastworks, and he was pierced with seven bullets.

Historical marker at the site of the Carter family's cotton ginhouse, Franklin, Tenn. (Photo Lochlainn Seabrook)

I have seen it stated, as coming from a Federal officer who was in command on that portion of the line, that they could have captured Gen. Adams, but had to kill him to check his brigade, or else his men would have captured the works. He said he was the bravest man he ever saw. His troops were always willing to follow him, having implicit confidence in his skill and generalship. History has never done him justice, and I hope Tennesseans will see to it that the page that records his deeds is one of the brightest that adorns Southern history, for she never gave the South a truer, better, or braver officer.

I hope to meet the surviving members of his staff at Memphis. It is indeed a very great pleasure to meet loved comrades now after the lapse of nearly forty years and to talk over those days of hardship and sacrifices, not unmingled with much pleasure.[40] — CONFEDERATE COLONEL JAMES R. BINFORD

MEMORIES OF GENERAL JOHN ADAMS

☛ I never think of you [Confederate Captain Gibson] that I am not reminded of that dismal night after the fatal battle of Franklin. When we attempted to rescue the body of our lamented general, you remember we met near the railroad cut, Thomas Bradley, member of Company F, Fifteenth Mississippi Regiment, who had attempted to rescue some friend, but found it so hazardous he concluded not to venture farther, and tried to dissuade us from an attempt fraught with so much danger; but, seeing our determination not to heed his advice, he, like the brave boy he was, said: "Well, I will go back with you." Always since I have chided myself for being so persistent in pressing forward.

You remember that when we got among the dead and wounded piled upon each other I planned as to how we should proceed separately and cautiously, and whichever one should find the body should give a shrill whistle, and the others would go to the call.

John Adams, C.S.A.

A few minutes thereafter I came across a poor wounded fellow, who told me to bend down. He informed me that I was in great danger, that the "Feds" had just passed over him in force, and I could then hear them, after listening carefully; they could not have been over fifteen steps away. I moped about cautiously for a few minutes, looking over the bodies of this one and that one in the hope of finding the body of Gen. Adams. All at once they fired a continuous volley, and in retiring I came across you, wounded, and Bradley also.

You remember when we had gotten across the railroad how lustily he called for Collins. It was then I realized the danger, and felt that I was the cause of his getting wounded. I have felt glad, however, a thousand times that you both recovered from your wounds. Bradley died a few years back. He married and reared a nice family. A son of his is a prominent young lawyer in Water Valley. He and I often talked about you, and of the effort we made that night to rescue our dead heroes.

As a man, Gen. Adams was greatly above the ordinary in every sense, and a true friend of mine to the last. . . . No battle in the history of the world was so fatal as that of Franklin.[41] — CONFEDERATE CAPTAIN JOHN L. COLLINS (aide-de-camp to Gen. Adams)

BATTLE OF FRANKLIN REMEMBRANCES

Historic Franklin as it appears today from the public square looking south. The most deadly fighting at the Battle of Franklin took place a little less than a mile from here. (Photo Lochlainn Seabrook)

☞ After an interval of thirty-eight years since the turbulent days of the sixties, I have been much interested in revisiting the battlefields of Nashville, Franklin, and Chickamauga.

I wondered before coming upon those scenes if anything there would appear to me now as I remembered it when I left it beclouded with the smoke of battle so long ago. I cannot adequately express the sensation produced when I came upon the plains and stood in the midst of the hills, every rise and fall of the land true to memory. In reverie I was the youthful Confederate soldier again moving with swaying columns of men, realizing again that indescribable thrill and inspiration of battle which cannot be known except by experience. As all these memories came crowding upon me with such freshness, to realize the flight of the years agone, I must be reminded of my gray beard and that I am now the head of a family of nine sons, half of whom have already attained a stature greater than my own; and that the youthful Confederate soldier is only a memory of the past.

Arriving at Franklin, I presented letters of introduction, and am much indebted to Dr. Hanner and Mr. McCann for their courteous interest and painstaking in accompanying me over the battlefields. Driving out in the midst of the undulating fields, stretching out between the low ridge around the town and the low range of mountains a mile to the south, the entire field could be scanned at a single glance. The whole ground is familiar.

It is not my purpose to give a general description of the battle, which has so often been portrayed by abler pens, but only to write my own experience and that of the immediate command to which I belonged.

I was a member of the Forty-first Mississippi Regiment, Sharp's Brigade, Lee's Corps. As shown in the history of the battle, this division of the Southern army was held in reserve and not brought into the engagement until late. During the early hours of the battle we had been filing along the summit and on the sides of the low mountains in the background, our position all the while shifting farther to the left and gradually closing in nearer the conflict. From the hills on which we stood overlooking the bare plains, we had an unobstructed view of the battle. The rising ground circling around the little town, crowned with the enemy's earthworks and bristling with their artillery, was belching flash and flame of lurid fire, and smoking like the crater of a volcano and the unintermitting roar was like one vast explosion. The sun was sinking low into a crimsoned sunset, as if miraged by the flow of human blood from the battlefield. From our elevation we had seen our brave men in solid lines march into the dismal scene and seem to disappear as though they had gone down into the crater, and still the shot and shell from the enemy's unsilenced batteries came whizzing and screaming across the plains.

Now it came our time to advance. Our final approach was almost from the westward. The shadows of coming night had settled heavily around us just as we came in range of their rifles and nerved ourselves for the charge. We were ordered to omit the usual "yell," conceal our approach under cover of the darkness, and make a spirited dash for the works. My own path lay through the north edge of the famed "locust grove." Our progress was retarded by the brush which had been cut down. We clambered over, pulled through, or crawled under on hands and knees as best we could. We

"The rising ground circling around the little town, crowned with the enemy's earthworks and bristling with their artillery, was belching flash and flame of lurid fire."

reached the works just a little to the left of the Carter brick dwelling. An impression had obtained that there were some Southern troops in front of us, but when we came to the works we found the enemy there ready to greet us.

At once there was a fierce struggle across the embankment as to which should hold the ground. Our approach under cover of the darkness had somewhat favored us. Gen. Jacob H. Sharp, commanding the brigade, says in a recent letter: "We were perhaps within thirty paces of the enemy's works when the darkness was lighted up as if by electric display. Then our brave men gave the yell and dashed into the works and stayed there until the enemy left."

As stated, our first clash was a fierce struggle across the works, at the very muzzle of our guns, as to which should hold the ground, and for a time (it appeared a long time) our fate seemed to tremble in the balance. At length the enemy in our immediate front were forced back, and the flag of the Forty-first Mississippi Regiment was borne across the works to the pursuit some distance to the front, a squad of us aligning ourselves with our colors. Our color bearer was E. L. Russell, then a youth of seventeen, sprightly, strong, and courageous, now Col. E. L. Russell, of Mobile, general counsel of Mobile and Ohio Railroad. He writes me in a recent letter: "Well do I remember what might be termed the lurid night in the locust thicket in front of Franklin. You are correct in your recollection: I carried the colors that evening and that night and went over the breastworks with four or five of the regiment at two different times."

The rally for advance was not general, and we returned under cover of the embankment. The enemy again returned to contest for the works, and this time we were there ready to greet them. There was a brief but fierce clash again, and another shout for an advance. Captain Spooner, of the Forty-first, mounted the works and walked to and fro, waving his sword and encouraging his men. His symmetric form could be seen through the darkness by the light from the perpetual flash of the guns. This was the second time our colors went over, as alluded by Col. Russell. This time (I think it was Ensign Russell) assisted me to bring a cartouch of ammunition, left by the enemy, across to our side. This gave us an abundant supply of ammunition, and we settled down to a steady fusillade to our front and left.

The Carter House, Franklin Tenn., as it looks today.
(Photo Lochlainn Seabrook)

While this fusillade seemed to hold the enemy at bay in our front, it brought us trouble from the left. We were on the extreme left. We were at a point where the works made a slight deflection to the northward, forming an obtuse angle. None of our men held the ground to our left beyond the point of this angle, while on the other side the ditch was filled with bluecoats just a few rods from us. Being on the outside of the angle gave us the advantage, as we could shelter under the works and pour an enfilade the down their line. This was too much for them, and one desperate effort after another was made by them to force their way up the ditch to our immediate front.

As we poured our deadly fire down their line, we could distinctly hear the death groan and agonizing cries of the wounded above the din of battle. The contest was thus continued for hours (it seemed an age), and we began to feel ourselves in great straits. We had been long without orders, not the voice of a commanding officer could be heard. We were hard pressed: what should we do? At this time, in an interval between the onslaughts, Capt. John Reed, commanding Company B, called a few heads close together to decide whether we should hold out, retreat, or surrender. The decision was made to fight to the bitter end.

The Masonic Temple, Franklin, Tenn. Built in 1823, at that time the three-story lodge was the tallest building west of the Allegheny Mountains. President Andrew Jackson's 1830 treaty with the Chickasaw Indians took place here, and during the Battle of Franklin in 1864 it was used as one of the town's many military hospitals. (Photo Lochlainn Seabrook)

General Sharp had been wounded; Colonel Simms and Colonel Smith had also been wounded; and Colonel Bishop was killed at the works, and the "High-Pressure Brigade" was without a commanding officer, and from that [moment] on, writes General Sharp, "it was managed by the company officers and the heroic men that were spared."

Late along toward midnight, as the firing began to slacken, and we "bitterly thought of the morrow," a bright flame broke out down in the town. We supposed they were evacuating, and burning what they could not carry away. We used this light to good advantage while it lasted. Every object was brought distinctly to view between us and this light. Their position was behind an inferior second line of works, a few rods in front of us. I saw a fellow pushing down a cartridge, saw the ramrod. I leveled my rifle till the outline darkened the sight and fired. I feel sure the ball he pushed never whistled by a Rebel's ear to make him dodge.

After this it became apparent that the enemy was not so aggressive. The firing slackened. There were intervals of complete silence again to be broken again by the crack of rifles. We placed certain of our men to keep watch over the works while the balance rested under cover, ready to spring to the defense at instant call. I remember the dramatic incident that drew out our last shots. A deathlike silence was pervading the hush of night, like the awe inspiring calm after a terrible storm, when a clear voice from one of our watchmen rang out: "Look at that Yankee right there!" Pop! pop!

pop! rang out a number of rifles. With the stealth of an Indian he had designed to creep upon us and give us a farewell shot, and was discovered within a few yards of our line. His life paid the forfeit for his folly. During all these long and dreadful hours, covered in the darkness of night, it was impossible for us to know what was going on any distance from us, or even to know the execution we were doing.

The Sweeny House, Gen. Hood's headquarters during the Battle of Franklin.

The coming of daylight revealed a gruesome sight. Our men who have bravely sacrificed their lives lay thick about the works and entangled in the locust brush. On the enemy's side to our left, where they had encountered our enfilade fire, their dead lay in a heap. There was a hunting for missing comrades. There was effort to reassemble shattered commands. Inquiry was made for commanding officers. All was found so depleted that it made the heart sink.

If it was a compliment to the Southern troops who fought at this point, that they held their ground by pouring a persistent deadly fire into the face of the enemy, it was an equal compliment to the brave Union men who disputed them to the last and received their fire.

Perhaps there was no part of the Confederate army that might not claim some special distinction. It was the distinction of the Forty-first Mississippi Regiment that, in all its long list of battles fought, it was never led to the charge without moving the enemy. In one instance alone, at the battle of Murfreesboro, a part of this regiment was repulsed, and, when ordered to retreat, retired under fire. I happened to be with that part, and it would be hard to express that experience. This regiment was organized and disciplined into the service by Col. W. F. Tucker. No man of truer heart or braver spirit ever drew sword in battle.

The brigade, by its intrepid dash under the leadership of Gen. J. H. Sharp, had won the sobriquet of the "High-Pressure Brigade." Gen. S. D. Lee, the corps commander, in a speech before the Mississippi Legislature, alluded to General Sharp at Franklin in the following language: "He led his command through the famous locust thicket, that ordinarily a dog could not have gotten through; he led them to the breastworks of the enemy and engaged in a death struggle over them, the troops on each side bayoneting each other. He captured three stands of colors, the only Confederate trophies taken on the ensanguined field. He was equally gallant on other fields; but if there was none other but Franklin, his name should go down immortal in history as a hero who led a band of Mississippians, all of whom were heroes.

To a visitor the field of Franklin is so marked in feature that it is recognized at every point; but many things on the scene to-day are in marked contrast with the day when "red battle stamped its foot" and the mountains trembled under thunders of war.

On an eminence to the south of the contested battle line, overlooking the entire field, there is now being erected a handsome, substantial school building to be known as Battlefield Academy. This school was formerly

located at the site of the Carter ginhouse, a point behind the line of works held by the Union troops. It was consumed by fire [in 1902], and is now being rebuilt on ground over which Confederates charged, as if ominous fate had augured that the youth of the South should be educated on soil baptized alone with the blood of the Southern. Smiling cottages dot the plain, bespeaking the abode of happy families. The genial sun warms the tranquil plain. "The warrior has turned his sword into pruning hooks. The farmer drives his team afield. And every sound of life is full of glee, from the merry mocking bird's song to hum of bee."

Cannonball memorial at the site of the cotton ginhouse, Franklin, Tenn. (Photo Lochlainn Seabrook)

My apology to my comrades for having attempted to write this, my remembrances of Franklin, is I am impressed that whatever of the true story of the South has not been told must be told by the few that remain of the rank and file before they depart, and truly the evening shadows are growing long, and it is time to make the record.[42] — CONFEDERATE PRIVATE GEORGE W. SEAWELL (41st Mississippi Regiment)

DRIVING YANKEES FROM THE FIELD AT FRANKLIN

☛ I was a member of Capt. J. E. Simmons' Company A, 3rd Mississippi Regiment, Featherston's Brigade, Army of Tennessee. Capt. Simms would always give his company a big dinner of pork and potatoes once a year when it was possible for him to do so. He was loved by his men. At the battle of Franklin he said to me, as we were going into the charge, November 30, 1864, "Dan, I will beat you to those yankees over yonder." Says I, "Captain, I will get there by the time you do."

The first line of works was soon reached. I fired my gun at the enemy as they were leaving these works, and was reloading when I saw our Captain on the works waving his hat to his company to "come on." He leaped off of the works and called to his company, "Come on, my brave boys, let's drive them from the field!" He went over the main line of works at the gin house and was captured. I was wounded in the hip just at their abatis.

The smoke soon settled on us with the darkness, so we could only see by the light of the guns. Our flag bearer was killed on their works. The enemy got the flag. If the old regiment could get our flag returned to them it would be a pleasure to have it at our reunions.[43] — CONFEDERATE SOLDIER D. J. WILSON (Era, Tex.)

FIVE DEAD CONFEDERATE GENERALS ON THE PORCH

☛ [Introduction to the entry following this one:] Fifty-eight years have passed since the battle of Franklin, Tenn., but the memory of it dieth not with those who took part in that bloody sacrifice, nor passes the memory of the kind ministrations rendered by the people of that unfortunate little

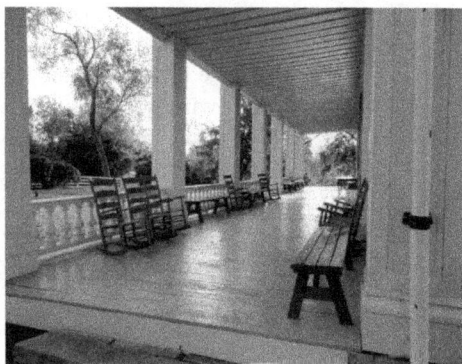

The deck of the rear portico, Carnton Plantation, Franklin, Tenn. Here the corpses of five Confederate generals were laid out after the Battle of Franklin, then the home of John and Carrie McGavock. A sixth Confederate general later died of his wounds, making this conflict one of the most extraordinary in recorded history. (Photo Lochlainn Seabrook)

town. Among the list stands out the name of Mrs. John McGavock [Caroline "Carrie" E. Winder] as the "Good Samaritan" of that battle, loved and revered for her devoted and unselfish service to the sick and wounded. The following article, by Dr. N. E. Morris, of Franklin, will be appreciated, especially by those who received the ministrations of this good woman:

"Those who have visited the battle field of Franklin recall the beautiful old Southern mansion that stands upon that historic ground. It was at the time of the battle the home of Col. John McGavock and his wife, Caroline Elizabeth Winder McGavock. They were both true types of the old-time Southerners, warm in heart, genial in manner, refined in sentiment, abundant in kindness.

"The position of 'Carnton,' so called for the old McGavock home in Ireland, would have caused the names of its occupants to be linked with that battle even had not their acts of mercy and loving service indissolubly associated them with the Confederacy. But no list of heroines of the war would the veterans in that engagement recognize as complete without the name of Mrs. McGavock. The home was filled with the wounded, and on the morning after the battle five Confederate generals lay dead on the wide gallery about the house."[44] — DR. N. E. MORRIS (Franklin, Tenn.) [See the following entry.]

"THE GOOD SAMARITAN OF WILLIAMSON COUNTY"

☞ I have now one more scene to paint, one more story to tell you, and I am done. I wish I had a pen to do justice to the subject, for in all the annals of war, filled as it is with the great and noble deeds of great and noble women, none exceed and few equal in true merit the noble sympathy of Mrs. John McGavock [née Caroline E. Winder].

When day dawned we found ourselves near her house [Carnton Plantation]—on her lawn—which was in the rear of our line. The house is one of the large old-fashioned houses of the better class in Tennessee, two stories high, with many rooms, and every arrangement for comfort.[45] This was taken as a hospital,

Facade, Carnton Plantation, Franklin, Tenn. (Photo Lochlainn Seabrook)

and the wounded, in hundreds, were brought to it during the battle, and all the night after. Every room was filled, every bed had two poor, bleeding fellows, every spare space, niche, and corner under the stairs, in the hall, everywhere—but one room for her own family. And when the noble old house could hold no more, the yard was appropriated until the wounded and the dead filled that, and all were not yet provided for. Our doctors were deficient in bandages, and she began by giving her old linen, then her towels and napkins, then her sheets and tablecloths, then her husband's shirts and her own undergarments.

During all this time the surgeons plied their dreadful work amid the sighs and moans and death rattle. Yet, amid it all, this noble woman, the very impersonation of divine sympathy and tender pity, was active and constantly at work. During all the night neither she nor any of the household slept, but dispensed tea and coffee and such stimulants as she had, and that, too, with her own hands. Unaffrighted by the sight of blood, unawed by horrid wounds, unblanched by ghastly death, she walked from room to room, from man to man, her very skirts stained in blood, the

Mrs. Carrie McGavock.

incarnation of pity and mercy. Is it strange that all who were there praise her and call her blessed?

When the war was over, Colonel [John] McGavock gave the ground for the cemetery, in which are gathered the bodies of the heroic soldiers who fell on that fatal field. On that spot nearly two thousand Confederate soldiers lie buried. The cemetery was called for the beloved husband, and the care of it was one of Mrs. McGavock's greatest delights.

It was to her thoughtfulness and oversight that a full list of the dead that rests there was made. She had a true record, and always kept it in her own possession.

Until the close of her life no sign of neglect showed in any part of the cemetery, it being her chief pleasure to see that no stray weeds crept upon the hallowed ground, and that the grass and inclosures showed in their careful keeping the love she bestowed upon that spot. She died at the home [Windermere] of her son-in-law, Mr. George L. Cowan [of Forrest's Escort], which stands on part of the original farm. The prayer offered by Rev. John W. Hanner on the occasion of her funeral so beautifully embodies the spirit that actuated her life that a part of it is quoted:

"We thank thee for the pilgrimage of thy handmaiden through this world, a pilgrimage guided by God, inspired by his spirit, and blessed by his Son, a pilgrimage which perfected the pilgrim and blessed her fellows on the right hand and on the left. We thank thee that she was a stranger to all that was unchildlike toward God and to all that was unsisterly toward mankind, a stranger to unloveliness and unkindness; but we thank thee that she was not a stranger to faith and hope and love, not a stranger to friendship, benevolence, and charity. We bless thee that through thy Spirit her heart was full of compassion, her hand ever open to the needy, and her feet ever ready to run errands of love and mercy. We thank thee for the hands which hung down and the feeble knees that she lifted up, for the many hearts she comforted, the needy ones she supplied, the sick she ministered unto, and the boys she found in abject want and mothered and reared into worthy manhood [it was Carrie's custom to take in orphan boys]. In the last day they will rise up and 'call her blessed.' To-day she is not, because thou hast taken her; and we are left to sorrow for the 'Good Samaritan of Williamson County,' a name richly merited by her."[46] — CONFEDERATE CAPTAIN WILLIAM DUDLEY GALE (written to his wife Katherine Polk Gale, daughter of Confederate Gen. Leonidas Polk)

SECTION 2

UNION
RECOLLECTIONS

"It was now four o'clock, and to the amazement of the thousands who were watching them, Wagner's infantry opened fire."

Union Recollections

GEN. SCHOFIELD'S REFLECTIONS ON THE BATTLE

John M. Schofield, U.S.A.

☛ The purpose of the operations of the Union troops, preceding and including the battle of Franklin, was not by any means to secure a safe retreat of the troops under my command and their junction with the force of [Union] Gen. [George H.] Thomas at Nashville. Nothing could have been easier than that. But the all important object was to retard the advance of Gen. Hood's army until Gen. Thomas could concentrate his troops at Nashville. The time actually gained at Columbia, Spring Hill and Franklin, was barely sufficient. Gen. A. J. Smith's corps was landing at Nashville during the battle of Franklin, and General Steadman's troops, from Chattanooga, did not arrive until the day after; indeed, some of them were cut off by Forrest's calvary. Gen. Hood, on the other hand, designed to cut off or crush my command before I could unite with Gen. Thomas. This, in my judgment, fully justified his direct assault in front at Franklin, for which some have criticised him. He did not have time to turn that position before our concentration at Nashville would be effected. Hence, he had no alternative but the desperate one of a direct assault.[47] — UNION GENERAL JOHN M. SCHOFIELD

FIGHTING WITH "THE FEROCITY OF DEMONS"

☛ Gen. Schofield, arriving [in Spring Hill] at this time [early morning, November 30, 1864] from Thompson's Station, ordered an immediate march to Franklin, and Gen. Cox's Division to lead the advance. Keeping up the long, steady stride of four miles an hour, in the clear starlight, without meeting a soul on the road, we reached Winstead Hills about 3 o'clock in the morning.[48]

The General and staff then pushed on rapidly to Franklin, awoke Col. Carter, and made headquarters at his little brick cottage, the last house in the southern suburbs of the town [of Franklin], on the Columbia pike.

In the absence of the Inspecting Officer, who was with the rearguard, the writer was instructed to place the troops in position; and while sitting out in front of the house, waiting for the head of column to arrive, everything was as still as the grave, and there was time to ponder on what the following day would bring forth.

I did not realize, and very few, perhaps, anticipated, the dreadful and bloody outcome; but, rather, looked for another flank movement, as at Columbia. Presently the tramp of horses in the distance and the rattle of tin cups against bayonet clasps foretold the coming of the troops. First the brigade officers, mounted, appeared, and they were led off to the right of the road, where a hasty inspection of the ground was made in the darkness; then the weary men came marching by the left flank. The night tramp had been wearing to those on foot, for they had been pressed to unusual speed, and their anxiety about the train, that was strung along by their side, kept them peering out into the dim distance, lest Forrest's cavalry might strike them at any point, although every regiment had a company deployed in the fields to our right. The Third Division of the Twenty-third Corps was led into position on the east side of the pike—Stiles, commanding Henderson's Brigade, first, Casement next, and Riley last, all facing the south. Col. Henderson was temporarily unwell, and had requested Col. Stiles, of the 63rd Ind., to relieve him of personal command of his brigade; but he remained with the brigade during the engagement, and watched every movement with as much solicitude as though he were giving the orders direct to the regimental commanders. Gen. Cox was placed in command of the two divisions, his own and Rugers, and was instructed—as soon as the troops could get a short breathing spell, a few winks of sleep, and their morning coffee—to strongly intrench themselves.

It was deemed expedient by Gen. Schofield to make our stand on the south side of the town and river, so that the trains could mass in the streets and open spaces in the village,

Historical marker at Fort Granger, Union stronghold during the Battle of Franklin. (Photo Lochlainn Seabrook)

while a wagonroad bridge was being built and planks laid on the sleepers of the railroad bridge for their transfer across. Gen. Schofield had the previous day sent an urgent request to Thomas to ship by rail a pontoon bridge to Franklin for the Harpeth crossing, and expected to find it there, but in this was disappointed. It had instead been sent by the wagonroad, in charge of Maj. Jenny, of the Engineer Corps, and did not arrive in time to be of service.

In this embarrassing situation there was nothing to do but construct the bridges with the meager facilities at hand; so, with his Engineer Battalion and details of troops, the work was performed, requiring his constant personal attention. He remained in this position up to the time of the engagement, so as to better superintend the crossing, and at the same time be near the railroad and telegraph station; while from Fort Granger, on the bluff east of the railroad and near the river, he had perfect command during the battle of the entire field, and to direct the fire of the artillery stationed there with him. During the forenoon the [Union] troops, in close order, kept pouring in, the infantry on the right side of the road and wagon trains and artillery to their left.

Famous "Forrest Crossing" at the Harpeth River, situated on the far right at the Battle of Franklin. It was here that Gen. Forrest and his men skirmished with Union troops along the waterway, while the main battle was being conducted about two miles to the northeast (right). The Winstead-Breezy Hill range, Hood's initial observation post, can be seen along the horizon at the back right. (Photo Lochlainn Seabrook)

The [Union] march was not so rapid as during the night, for they were continually harassed by Forrest's cavalry attaching in weak points on the road. [Thomas J.] Wood's Division of the Fourth Corps passed through the town and formed in position on the north of the Harpeth; Kimball's Division of the same corps was ordered to report to Gen. Cox, and was placed by him on the right of the Twenty-third Corps, with its right flank resting on the Harpeth River. Two brigades of Wagner's Division, Fourth Corps (Lane's and Conrad's), were countermarched, and placed something over 100 rods in our front, across the Columbia pike, to watch the approach of the enemy, and to their right and front, on a little knoll, a section of Marshall's Battery, supported by an infantry regiment.

Opdycke's Brigade, of the same division, which had been acting as rearguard from Spring Hill, passed through our line, and was ordered by Gen. Cox to take up position in reserve behind Carter's Hill. The two regiments of Reilly's Brigade that were left back in the skirmish line at Duck River arrived, and formed the second line behind the main works. The batteries of the Fourth Corps were placed in our main line. They were ordered to report to Gen. Cox, to take the places of the Twenty-third Corps artillery that had been posted on the north side of the river, as it was the first on the ground, and it was the intention, at that hour, to have all the artillery pass over as it arrived. By the middle of the afternoon our trains were nearly all across the river, and it was intended the troops should follow after dark, and accompanying them during the night toward Nashville. But it seemed that Gen. Schofield's plans were to be somewhat interfered with, to the extent that the continuation of our march was some hours later.

For when Gen. Hood's sleepy army awoke at Spring Hill, and he found how skillfully Gen. Schofield had marched his command past him during the night, and an examination by daylight showed him how easily he could have cut us in two at any time during the night or headed us off entirely the previous afternoon, had he known our exact situation, he was so chagrined that he cursed everybody, high and low; censured Cheatham and Cleburne, and the entire forces that were present, for not taking possession of the road; and made his whole army understand that it must make up for that blunder at once, and that no time was to be lost in overtaking and destroying our army wherever found. So he pushed on in pursuit, their cavalry occasionally attacking our trains and burning a wagon or two, until they came up with our rearguard about noon at Winstead Hills. These two splendid fighting Generals, Cheatham and

Present-day view from the top of 840-foot tall Winstead Hill, overlooking Columbia Avenue (center) and the plain of Franklin. It was here that Hood identified Union positions and planned his movements. The site is now a Confederate memorial park dedicated to Southern soldiers who fought in the Battle of Franklin. Engraved stone markers honoring some of the Confederate officers who perished as a result of the conflict can be seen in the lower right. (Photo Lochlainn Seabrook)

Cleburne, felt keenly the morning's reprimand, which they considered undeserved, and as they rode together at the head of their commands they discussed it with bitter resentment, and determined at the first opportunity to make the fight of their lives, and disprove the unjust charges of their commander. Stewart's Corps moved on to the right, toward Lewisburg pike, turning Opdycke's flank, when he fell slowly back to the town.

Gen. Cheatham with his corps moved by the Columbia pike, and formed in line north of Winstead Hills. From our position the [Confederate] officers and horses could be plainly seen on this range of hills, a little more than two miles away, as though studying our position.

From this elevation the beautiful panorama, embracing the rolling intervening country and the town of Franklin nestling in the Valley of the Harpeth, was plainly in the vision of Hood's officers, showing also the disposition of our troops and the earthworks encircling the town. Bate's Division marched over to Carter's Creek pike and formed behind the Bostwick house. Stewart's Corps moved over to the McGavock house, where the first skirmish firing was heard in the grove; it was by [James W.] Reilly's men, who had gone there for logs to put on the earthworks.

Firing was now commenced over on the right where Bate was forming, and the guns stationed on the pike poured in volley after volley with great rapidity. Gen. Cox rode over to Henderson's Brigade, which was on higher ground, and from a parapet, with his field glass, watched the advancing lines until they ran over Wagner's men.

George D. Wagner, U.S.A.

He then mounted his horse and pushed for the center, steadying the line and directing the men to withhold their fire until the advanced lines were inside of the works. The suspense was now growing, for we knew there was to be a battle. The men were heated from the exertion of strengthening the works, but they laid down their shovels and picks, and took up their guns with a firm grip, and stood there with bated breath and blazing eyes, frowning over the works at the advancing foe and awaiting the order to commence firing; for they were fairly burning to avenge the deaths of their brave comrades that were left on the bloody battlefields of northern Georgia, and this was their first good chance for wiping out many an old score; and, oh! what a real comfort it was to know that we who, during the hot Summer campaign, had stood the crash of so many fierce assaults against their solid fortifications, were now on the right side of the works, and in such a splendid position, with a gentle slope away from us and not even a mullein-stalk to obstruct our fire for a good third of a mile.

Before the break in the advanced lines, Gen. Cox's Engineer Officer, the writer, was standing on the parapet of the 100th Ohio, the first one on the left of the Columbia pike, urging the men to strengthen the works, and talking with Gen. Wagner at the time. The General was reclining on his elbow, his feet hanging over the works, with a staff or crutch in his hand; he had fallen with his horse and was lame. They remarked that the musketry firing was becoming more rapid, also that the section of artillery was doing some lively work. By and by a staff officer rode fast from one of the brigades and reported to Wagner, excitedly, "The enemy are forming in heavy columns; we can see them distinctly in the open timber and all along our front." Wagner said firmly: "Stand there and fight them." Then turning to the Engineer Officer, he said, "And that stubbed, curly-headed Dutchman will fight them, too." Meaning one of his brigade commanders. "But, General," the Engineer said, "the orders are not to stand, except against cavalry and skirmishers, but to fall back behind the mainline if a general engagement is threatened."

In a short time another officer of Stanley's staff rode in from the right in great haste and told him the rebels were advancing in heavy force. He received the same order. The officer added: "But Hood's entire army is coming." Then Wagner struck the ground with his stick. "Never mind; fight them." But even after this, they had time to come back in good order if they had been so directed.

Soon we heard the rebel yell and heavy firing. Marshall's men with the two guns had fixed prolonge and fired as they fell back on the pike to the advanced rifle pits, leaving their dead, but bringing in their wounded. The horses then brought the guns in

"Soon we heard the rebel yell and heavy firing. It was now continuous. Old hell was letting loose."

on an easy trot. As they turned in around the short apron earthwork covering the gap across the pike, Alec Clinton, one of the gunners, jumped off the limber, his face black with powder smoke, and said, with a grim smile, "Old hell is let loose, and coming out there."

The firing now was continuous, and under the rising smoke we could see a commotion in our advanced brigades; officers were hurrying from point to point to hold the men to their work. A few horsemen were in sight, some mounting and others dismounting, but only an occasional dropping back. Soon we noticed the right of Stewart's command wrapping around [Joseph] Conrad's left, and then our men rose up and the break commenced. The right of Cheatham's corps was sweeping over the little rise of ground on which the low earthworks were built, in what appeared a solid human wave. And such a racket! Their shouting seemed to show such confidence as men who have been led to believe that the line they were assaulting was a weak one. The firing had slackened and the smoke cleared, so that we could plainly see the splendid advance.

It was a grand sight! Such as would make a lifelong impression on the mind of any man who could see such a resistless, well-conducted charge. For the moment we were spellbound with admiration, although they were our hated foes; and we knew that in a few brief moments, as soon as they reached firing distance, all of that orderly grandeur would be changed to bleeding, writhing confusion, and that thousands of those valorous men of the South, with their chivalric officers, would pour out their life's blood on the fair fields in front of us. As forerunners well in advance could be seen a line of wild rabbits, bounding along for a few leaps, and then they would stop and look back and listen, but scamper off again, as though convinced that this was the most impenetrable line of beaters-in that had ever given them chase; and quails by the thousands in covies here and there would rise and settle, and rise again to the warm sunlight that called them back; but, no, they were frightened by the unusual turmoil, and back they came and this repeated until finally they rose high in the air and whirred off to the gray skylight of the north.

The day had been bright and warm, reminding us of the Northern Indian Summer; the afternoon sun, like a ball of fire, was settling in all its southern splendor in a molten sea of bronze, over the distant hills; and in the hazy, golden light, and with their yellowish-brown uniforms, those in the front ranks seemed to be magnified in size; one could almost imagine them to be phantoms sweeping along in the air. On they came, and in the center their lines seemed to be many deep and unbroken, the red-and-white tattered flags, with the emblem of St. Andrew's cross, as numerous as though every company bore them, flaring brilliantly in the sun's rays, with conspicuous

Edward R. S. Canby, U.S.A.

mounted groups of general and staff officers in their midst, and a battery or two in splendid line charging along between the divisions. Scattered along in front of them were our men bent almost to the ground, with their heads turned to see if the enemy were gaining on them. It was every man for himself and the devil take the last man over the works; but here and there brave fellows would hesitate as if they would like to face and fight them.

On the right of Walthall's and the left of Loring's Divisions there were occasional breaks made by our infantry and the terrific volleys from the batteries on the opposite bank of the river; also, from Marshall's and Canby's Battery M, 4th U. S. Art., who poured canister into the enemy that were swarming through the railroad cut; but officers on horseback and afoot were at every gap, trying to close them up, so that, on the left, Stewart's living sea, with raging surf, in wave following wave, broke and fell, and plunged onward over the sloping beach in our front.

Those who have stood on the Cliff road at Newport [Rhode Island] and watched the masses of brown seaweed from the gulf stream carried by the white-capped waves over the bright green water of the beach will have a fair idea of the appearance of those lines that charged forward and receded on that fateful day. Still the great seething mass came rolling on to our center.

"The Confederates, in wave following wave, broke and fell, and plunged onward over the slope in our front."

Although the smoke was spreading, we could see them plainly, but could not open with our artillery and infantry fire until our men were safely over. It was a situation that required the greatest bravery for the men to stand there firmly, and to hold their fire until the enemy were within 100 yards of our intrenchments. But those stern-faced veterans from the Middle West, in regiments that were short, though compact, touched elbows and grappled grimly their trusty Enfields, ready to pour in their first volley as soon as the Fourth Corps men uncovered their front.

Oh, what a mistake the brave Wagner made! Through the gap, at last, and over the works our men came, with Cleburne and Brown hot after them. Wagner by this time was on his horse riding backward and facing the disorganized [Union] brigades, trying as hard as ever a man did to rally them. With terrible oaths he called them cowards, and shook his broken stick at them; but back they went to the town, and nothing could stop them. The writer was also mounted and assisted Wagner until, in front of the Carter House, he was so unfortunate as to be dismounted, receiving a slight wound in the leg from the same shot that killed his horse. Just then a young sergeant, all made up of true mettle, and with flashing eye, turned and brought his gun down on the ground and said: "Hold on, boys; I don't go back another step." About 20 stopped with him. I patted him on the back and led him with his men into our reserve line; perhaps others stopped, but the great mass went through the town and across the river.

Wagner was a great fighter; it is said that bullets rattled out of his clothes for a month after the battle of Stone's River, and his division was as good as any other, but they had been pressed too closely, and for some reason thought the whole line would break. Their officers tried hard to check them, but their organization was broken in their scramble back from the front. It was not the fault of the men, nor their officers, but of their rash

General, and it was the only fault in his long, splendid career; but it lost him his command. Poor Wagner is now dead; his soul is in Heaven with the heroes, and let us exercise our full measure of charity in forgiving this one error, and cherish the memory of his personal valor and dauntless courage on the hard-fought battlefields of the West.

If our men, in this part of the line, with every fiber strained to almost breaking tension, could have had time to fire two or three volleys, they would have regained the nerve they had lost during this awful suspense, and held the line without a waver. But Cheatham's whole corps was right on top of those few regiments before they could fire a shot, and some of them were forced back a short distance from the line on either side of the pike. Now was the great opportunity for the brave Cols. Rousseau and White and the battery commander, Charley Scoville. The two former were in command of Reilly's second line and had been cautioned by Gen. Cox, before riding over to Henderson's Brigade, to look out for a break at this point, and when it did come they were ready. These troops were made up of those daring, earnest men from the mountains of East Tennessee and Kentuckians from the northeastern part of the State, where they were so thoroughly loyal that they kept on shooting rebels after the war was over.[49] They did not wait for an order, but sprang over the low rifle-pits like tigers, and with a shrill shout that was heard even above the rebel yell, and a heroism rarely equalled by men, went pell-mell into the mass of Confederates that had taken our line and did not know what to do with it. At the same time Charley Scoville cracked his blacksnake whip around the ears of his artillerymen, and drove them back to the guns. At it they went with pick-axes and shovels, slashing all around them with the ferocity of demons.

Jacob D. Cox, U.S.A.

For a few minutes there was a fierce hand-to-hand combat, and it was right in those few minutes that the fate of one or the other of the armies was to be decided. For a little time it looked decidedly against us, but the desperate determination of our men, who were rallying to regain the line, had its effect, and a change began to show itself.

A moment before Gen. Cox had sent Lieut. Tracy, one of his aides, to order up Opdycke's Brigade, but they were already filing up the pike, left in front, with their chivalric chief on foot by their side. Gen. Cox led them diagonally across the pike, so as to uncover the buildings in Carter's yard, preparatory to charging the broken line in [Silas A.] Strickland's front. They were pointed directly toward the place Rousseau and White were engaged, and the Confederates took it for a heavy reinforcement of that part of the line. One by one they seemed shaken, feeling that they were to be overpowered; and, not wishing to place themselves again in our front, they threw down their arms and rushed to our rear, prisoners without a guard.

When Opdycke's men faced to the front to charge the line, it was a more serious undertaking, as a larger number of men had broken over the works at this point, and had obtained a firmer footing. But there was nothing too alarming for Opdycke's bravery, and he urged his men forward, placing himself where he could prevent stragglers from dropping out. He broke his revolver over men's heads, and then seized a gun, and whoever looked back within his reach was jobbed under the blouse. So he rushed them on, and forced Brown's men from the outbuildings in Carter's yard. Strickland's men rallying, counter-charged and joined him and soon the ground was in our possession again, and a second line established.

Gen. Cox remained mounted during the entire engagement, so as to carefully watch the whole line; and while the confusion was greatest, during the break, he was in the midst, displaying heroic bravery, with hopeful look and sword poised above. The men saw his conspicuous figure, rallied around him, and he waved them back to the line. His sublime courage was an inspiration, and the

Samuel E. Opdycke, U.S.A.

weakest man in his command could not withstand its influence. If ever an example of personal bravery turned a tide of battle, surely at this point Gen. Cox's quiet but superb magnetism impelled every man who caught his eye to redoubled effort in wresting victory from defeat. Gen. Stanley was also there, showing great gallantry in encouraging the troops, but was wounded before he had been on the field 10 minutes; his horse was shot under him and Gen. Cox dismounted his staff officer, Tracey, who was riding his heavy claybank horse, turning it over to Stanley who rode to the rear.

Every charge ordered by Hood, or any of his Generals, after this first dreadful avalanche crumbled and broke, was foolhardy and reckless. After our line was re-established it was as steady as a granite wall; it was next to impossible to break it, and the enemy could only get over our parapet as prisoners or by being killed in the attempt. The brave soldiers of the South felt it, too, for their after-charges, although started with a yell, were silent as they reached our furious sheets of flame, and as they were forced in their heads were bent, their hats pulled down, and their arms shielding from sight the almost certain death that awaited them.

It was the writer's pleasure, a few years since, while on a pilgrimage to the old battlefields, to meet at Nashville the late Gen. Cheatham, a very comfortable man to approach, with a make-up about equally divided between a well-to-do Southern farmer and a Prussian Field-Marshal, having a ruddy, full face and snow-white mustache. He greeted me most cordially, clasping me in his arms, and said: "Well, I heard you were here, and I've been looking all over for you. Welcome to Tennessee; any man who was in the battle of Franklin, no matter which side, is my friend." Then we had a good chat about old times. Referring to the two brigades out in front: "Ah," he said, "if it hadn't been for the mistake your side made there, you would have killed every man in our army, and God knows you killed enough of them." It is undoubtedly a fact that if the brigades had been called in at the right time, no part of our [Union] line would have been broken; and if all our brigades had heeded the precaution to place head-logs on our works, and abatised our front, as Casement's did, the loss all along the lines would have been as light as his, which was comparatively insignificant. The officers of Casement's Brigade had their men take timbers from the cotton-gin house at the right of the line, also cut trees from the grove, and carried the legs in to be placed on the top of the parapet. They rested on cross-ties hollowed out to receive them, leaving a three-inch space through which to fire.

Confederate soldiers charging the Union line with their hats pulled down over their eyes.

Henderson's Brigade, on our extreme left, reached to the railroad track, and the works were built in the grounds of a large mansion, which were bordered by a splendid osage-orange hedge.

The line was located about 50 feet from this hedge, so that by cutting off the trees about four feet above the ground it left an impenetrable obstruction, and at the same time open enough through which to fire. The tops were scattered along in front of Casement's Brigade, making one of the most deceptive rows of abatis ever formed; it was light, but an occasional crotched stick held it in place.

Walthall's men stopped when it was reached; they were bewildered; they couldn't get over it; they undertook to pull it away, but the sharp thorns pierced their hands, and they gave that up; then right in the smoke of our guns they faced to the right, and filed through a gap made by a wild charging horse. All this time death was pouring into them sheets of flame and lead from the three-inch gap under the head-logs. One company of the

65ᵗʰ Ind. had repeating Spencer rifles, and at that short range their execution must have been terrible.

Capt. [A. P.] Baldwin's battery was stationed at this point, where the dead were piled up like snowdrifts in Winter time, and here it was that the obstructions caused them to mass so many deep.

The brave Captain quickly took advantage of the situation, and to mow down this dense forest of humanity he loaded his guns to the muzzles with triple rounds of canister and dummies made with stockings which the gunners took from their feet, and filled with bullets from the infantry ammunition boxes. To use the Captain's words, "At every discharge of my gun there were two distinct sounds—first the explosion, and then the bones." What fearful carnage, where, at short range, such loads of iron and lead were driven through the living wall of men, that the crunching of the bones could be distinguished! It was the same battery

"What fearful carnage, where, at short range, such loads of iron and lead were driven through the living wall of men, that the crunching of the bones could be distinguished!"

that was saved while marching out of Spring Hill by the coolness of one of the non-commissioned officers. Orders had been given to try to push through on the Franklin pike, with instructions to abandon and destroy the guns, and to save themselves and horses by breaking off into the fields on the left, if attacked and hard-pressed.

They were halted by a rebel picket reserve, posted a short distance from the road, and the demand came out from the darkness: "What battery is you-uns?" The commander was about to reply by unlimbering and turning his guns upon them, when the quick thought struck one of his Corporals to say, in a careless voice, "Tenth Alabam. What reegiment is you-uns?" "Fourteenth Missipp," was the reply, and, apparently satisfied, the drowsy sentinel settled down in the fence-corner to sleep. They pushed on, and were not again molested until nearly daylight, when they were attacked by Hood's cavalry. "Battery by the left flank: Fire to the rear," was the Captain's prompt order. A half-dozen rounds of 12-pound solid shot scattered the cavalry and saved the trains of two corps.

After dark, when it was safe to look over the works, it was a ghastly sight to see the mangled dead. All along in front of Casement's line the bodies reminded one of a rail fence toppled over and crossed many deep; or as if grim death had built a new abatis of thickly-tangled boughs. The ditch at Fort Sanders, Knoxville, just one year before, where the pick of Longstreet's army lay writhing as thick as the sea lions on the cliff rocks near the Golden Gate was bad enough to look at, but this was horrible.

The groans and moanings were pitiable from the poor fellows who were so badly wounded that they could not move away. Here is where Gen. John Adams plunged through the abatis, cleared the ditch, and fell across the crest and headlog; the rider fell outside the line, with from 30 to 40 wounds. He was gently handled, and placed upon the ground inside the lines. This is where Jack [John S.] Casement stood when he made his great speech. When the approaching enemy was nearing our line he sprang upon the works and turned to his troops, and, with that noted ringing voice that every one could hear: "Men, do you see those damn rebel sons-of-bitches coming?" Then a shout went up. "Well, I want you to stand here like rocks, and whip hell out of them." He then faced about and fired his revolvers until they were empty, and jumped down with the men.

John S. Casement, U.S.A.

The oratory may not have been as elegant as though studied for the occasion, but Caesar to his Romans and Hannibal to his Carthagenians never made speeches thrilling their armies with more effect. It was what they understood and appreciated, and what they did afterwards showed how well it was heeded. Not one man left the line, and it was Col. Jack's example that held them to the firing line. As a commander of men he had no superior, having that magnetic influence which drew from them their full capacity of service. His look and command held them as firmly as the silken sashes that bound together the Greeks at the pass of Thermopylae.

Just at this time, when the Confederate line was close to our works, and our men were concealed by the head-logs, Jim Coughlan, a [Union] Lieutenant of the 24th Ky., and Gen. Cox's favorite aide, mounted his black horse, and, swinging his cavalry saber over his head, charged back and forth along the whole line, cheering the men, and they all turned and gave him a cheer, for every man knew the gallant officer. He is the one who, on the white horse, led every charge of the Twenty-third and Fourth Corps across the field on the first day at Resaca; and all through the Atlanta campaign just such brilliant achievements on his part were noticed. It was not his dashing gallantry alone that made him such a favorite, but his military genius was of the highest order, and he was ever ready and anxious for duty, with no thought of the weather or hour of the night. If there was a spice of danger in it, he was better suited. Often, to avoid the dullness of camp life, he has begged to accompany me on topographical trips, when it was necessary to get information about the country ahead of us.

He was always of the greatest assistance to me. But what risks he would take! It was my custom to approach a log hut or rail pile on the road cautiously and expose as little of myself and horse as possible; but he would gallop on ahead in the middle of the road, singing or whistling with the greatest glee, and there had to be more than two rebel cavalrymen stationed in the road to keep him from charging. When he mounted his horse at Franklin and rode off along the line, with his full figure exposed above the works, the staff officers remarked to each other that he would surely be killed. It was late at night when we found him near the cotton-gin, where the hand-to-hand fighting was the fiercest. We lifted the cape from his pale face, and the stars looked down with us and wept. He was a handsome fellow of 22 years, with intelligent blue eyes, classic features, and a trim brown beard that the contaminating razor had never touched. He was born in southern Illinois, of Irish parents. Previous to the war he found employment as a school teacher in Kentucky, and when his regiment was recruited he was one of the first to offer his services.

The ride to Nashville was lonely to me, and I expected, after three days and two nights without sleep, when we spread our blankets on the floor of a small house outside the lines, that slumber would come quickly; but it was not so with me. After supper I called my black [Yankee] servant [slave], Scott, to bring me a bucket of water, with which I swashed out my boot, that was plastered thick on the inside with foul mud made from the dust of the pike and

James Coughlan, U.S.A.

blood that trickled from two wounds that were not at all painful. After making myself as clean and comfortable as possible, I sat on the side of my bed and looked over to the empty half that my good friend Coughlan had occupied, and my only utterance was "Poor Jim." In my broken sleep I rolled over several times during the night, and the same sorrowful words escaped me. It made me wakeful, and I was broken with grief to think that I could not be with him while he was dying to hear his last request and give him my hand for his death-grip. Before daylight I got up and sat by the window, for the bed was so lonely. The one who had shared the blankets with me for nearly a year was back at the Harpeth River, near the bridge-head, with two feet of earth over him. This brave officer could see only one thing in martial glory, and that was to die in battle.

His mind had been usually bright and happy, but gloomy spells were coming oftener as the dread disease of epilepsy increased and blighted his future. The nights were more frequent, when, after one of these spasms, I gently rolled him back in bed.

Levi T. Scofield, U.S.A.

There was no suffering, and he had no recollection in the morning of what had occurred; but once in awhile a depressed feeling would prompt him to ask me if he had been unwell in the night, and I would satisfy him with a cheering word. We who knew him, when we saw him dead, believed that what he most dearly wished had come. Dying like a hero in one of the greatest battles of the world's history, before his mind became clouded and his system broken with bad health, was to him well treasured as his dearest prayer.

The Confederate drummer-boy who was killed while trying to block a cannon.

[One last thing:] During one of the charges that was made on this part of the line, an incident occurred at Scoville's battery which is worth relating. A slight [Confederate] boy of not more than 15 years, with drum on his back, belonging to one of the Missouri regiments, foolishly attempted to force his way through one of the embrasures and thrust a fence rail into the mouth of the cannon, thinking, by his brave act, to stop the use of that gun. It was heavily loaded at the time, and was fired, tearing the poor boy to shreds, so that nothing was ever found of him. [50] — UNION CAPTAIN LEVI T. SCOFIELD (23rd Army Corps)

THE UNION VIEW OF THE BATTLE OF FRANKLIN

☛ The march of the National [Union] army from Spring Hill to Franklin [during the early morning of November 30, 1864] was not seriously interrupted. [Confederate officer Nathan Bedford] Forrest's troopers made an occasional dash at the long wagon train, but only in one or two instances did they succeed in reaching it, and very few wagons were lost. After seeing his columns fairly started, Schofield rode forward and overtook General Cox [the writer of this entry] with the advanced division just before the village of Franklin was reached. He had, about noon, urgently renewed his request to Thomas to send a pontoon bridge to the crossing of the Harpeth River, but having received no answer, he spurred forward with his staff to see if it had arrived. It was not yet daybreak, and the division was ordered to mass by the roadside to allow the trains to pass into the town. The division commander and his staff had halted at the house of a Mr. Carter, at the edge of the village (a house soon to become the key-point of a fierce battle) and were trying to catch a few minutes' sleep upon the floor, when General Schofield returned, much disturbed at finding that no pontoons had come. He ordered General Cox to assume command of both divisions of the Twenty-third Corps, and, as soon as day should dawn, intrench them upon the best line which could be made right and left of the knoll on which the Carter house stood, to cover the crossing of the trains and the rest of the army. He himself, with Major Twining, his Chief Engineer, began immediately to plan such improvements of the river crossings as should enable him to get the trains and the artillery upon the north side of the Harpeth at the earliest possible hour.

Railroad bridge over the Harpeth River, Franklin, Tenn., as it looked around the turn of the 20th Century. The remnants of Fort Granger can be seen on the bluffs in the background.

The village of Franklin is upon the south side of the river, which partly encloses it in a deep curve to the northeast. The northern bank is here considerably higher than the other, and, upon a hill commanding the railway and wagon-road bridges, an earthwork called Fort Granger had been built more than a year before. The railway approaches the town from the south, parallel to the Columbia turnpike, and about five hundred yards east of it. For a thousand yards it runs close to the bank of the river and on the eastern edge of the village, then crosses without change of direction, for the river here makes a turn to the west, nearly at right angles to its former course. Through a part of the distance last traversed the railway is in a considerable cut, and this as well as the bridges and the reach of the river, is completely under the fire of the fort. The Carter's Creek turnpike runs southwest from the centre of the town.

The line selected for defence was a curve which would be very nearly that struck with a radius of a thousand yards from the junction of the two turnpikes in the village. Its centre was a few rods in front of the Carter house on the Columbia road, and was upon a gentle rise of ground. Its left was at the railway cut close to the river, where was another knoll. Upon this line the Carter's Creek turnpike is about the same distance from the Columbia turnpike as the railway, and this constituted the proper front facing Columbia and Spring Hill, whence Hood was advancing. The third division of the Twenty-third Corps (General Reilly in temporary command) was placed on the left, Reilly's own brigade resting its flank on the pike, with Casement's and Henderson's brigades (Colonel Stiles in temporary command of the latter) continuing the line to the railway and river. The front of Reilly's own brigade was shorter than the others, for the two regiments which were left behind as pickets at Duck River belonged to it, and these did not arrive till the line was occupied.

Historical marker, Carter House, Franklin, Tenn. The first name of Confederate Captain Theodrick "Tod" Carter—who was shot down within sight of his family home—is misspelled. (Photo Lochlainn Seabrook)

They were then placed in second line, supporting the first and less than a hundred yards in rear of it. [Thomas H.] Ruger's division was between the Columbia and Carter's Creek turnpikes, Strickland's brigade on the left, and Moore's on the right. Along the whole front the ground sloped very gently from the line, and was only obstructed by a small grove of locust trees a short distance in front of Ruger, and by farm buildings, with orchards here and there in the distance. A range of high hills bounded this plain on the south [known as the Winstead-Breezy Hill range], through a gap in which the Columbia road runs. The Twenty-third Corps immediately began the building of breastworks, and by noon a strong intrenchment had been completed, the lack of timber for revetment being the only thing which prevented it from being equal to those usually made during the campaign. An old cotton gin in Reilly's line furnished timber for head-logs, and upon the knoll near the railway, at the Carter house, and in one or two other places, where the slope was sufficient, strong epaulements for artillery were constructed inside of and somewhat higher than the infantry parapet. At the Columbia turnpike the full width of the road was left open, for it was all needed to enable the doubled lines of wagons and artillery to pass, and a retrenchment crossing the road a few rods in rear was built to command the opening and its approach.

At the river it had been found that by scarping the banks, the ford, though a very bad one, could be used to some extent. Some wooden buildings were dismantled to furnish planking for the railway bridge, and a wagon approach to this was made. The lower part of the posts of the county bridge were found to be good, and these were sawn off nearly level with the water, crossbeams and planking were laid upon them, and by noon the army was provided with two passable bridges. The artillery of the Twenty-third Corps passed over first of all at the ford, to gain time, and part of it was placed on the fort on the north bank, General Stanley being directed to send several batteries of the Fourth Corps to report to the commandant upon the line when they should arrive. The trench on the left, in front of Stiles, was placed close behind a thick-set hedge of osage orange, which was thinned out so as to make an impassable thorny palisade, and the material was used to make a slight obstruction in front of Reilly's brigades. In front of Ruger the locust grove was cut down for the same use, though the trees were much too small for the purpose. At General Cox's request for troops to cover the right flank, since his force was not sufficient to reach the river on that side, Kimball's division of the Fourth Corps was ordered to report to him as it came in, and was placed there.

Wood's division of the Fourth Corps arrived and crossed to the north bank, Kimball had taken his place in the line, Wilson's cavalry was upon Wood's left, opposing the efforts of Forrest to cross the river in that direction, the town was full of wagons waiting their turn at the bridges, and some of them struggling through the ford. The wearied troops, which had fought and marched since daybreak of the preceding day, dropped to sleep as soon as their breastworks were built, and caught such rest as they could preparatory to a more terrible struggle and another night of marching.

On the Confederate side, [S. D.] Lee had sent forward the artillery from Columbia, as soon as it could be crossed over Duck River in the morning, and with it went ammunition for Forrest's men, who were getting short of it. The march in pursuit does not seem to have been hurried, and the single

Thomas J. Wood, U.S.A.

brigade, which was rear-guard, had no difficulty in holding back the enemy. A more annoying task was to drive forward the stragglers. A number of new regiments had joined the army at Columbia, and in these were many inexperienced recruits, who were not hardened to their work, and who had overloaded their knapsacks. It required the utmost exertion to prevent these men from falling into the enemy's hands, footsore and dispirited from fatigue as they were. To keep them up, Colonel Opdycke was obliged to order their knapsack straps to be cut, and to detail a provost guard to hurry them on.

Nathan B. Forrest, C.S.A.

About noon the [Union] rear-guard reached the hills at the border of the Harpeth Valley, from which the heavy columns of Hood's army could now be seen advancing rapidly. Opdycke checked them for a time by opening upon them with artillery, but was then withdrawn and brought within the lines, where he was placed in reserve upon the west of the Columbia road, two or three hundred yards from the Carter house. Wagner placed the rest of his division (Lane's and Conrad's brigades) astride the Columbia turnpike, about half a mile in front of the principal line. The commandant upon the line was notified by General Schofield that Wagner's orders directed him to remain in observation only till Hood should show a disposition to advance in force, and then to retire within the lines to Opdycke's position and act as a general reserve. Wagner, on being shown the note conveying this notice, said that such were his orders.

By three o'clock the trains were nearly all over the river, and Schofield had issued orders that the troops should also pass over at six o'clock if the enemy should not attack before sunset. But the period of depression and recrimination in Hood's army in the morning seems to have been followed by fierce excitement. Cleburne talked with Brown, as they rode along, complaining bitterly that Hood had censured him, and telling of his determination to demand an investigation. Evidently all were keyed to a high moral tension, and were determined that at the next opportunity, their commander should not have it to say that his plans had failed from any lack of energy or courage on their part. Hood, himself, had resolved upon a desperate effort to destroy Schofield's army before any further concentration of Thomas's forces could be made. About three o'clock word was sent from Wagner's brigades in front that the enemy was forming at the foot of the hills in heavy force, and reiterating to General Wagner the directions already given him, the commandant upon the line went to the knoll in Stiles's brigade, which afforded a better view of the whole field. General Schofield had moved his headquarters to the north side of the river, and was personally at the fort on the hill, which not only commanded a view of the field, but was nearest the bridges by which communication was kept up, and where alone he could see the cavalry demonstrations on the left where Forrest and Wilson were already engaged. The village itself is on a

The 1858 Lotz House, Franklin, Tenn. On November 30, 1864, prior to the battle, the family, headed by German immigrant Johann Albert Lotz, took shelter across the street at the Carter House. (Photo Lochlainn Seabrook)

plateau lower than the line intrenched, and from it nothing whatever could be seen. General Stanley, who had been ill during the morning, had also his quarters on the north of the Harpeth, with Wood's division.

A depression in front of Wagner's brigades and some scattered trees shut out Hood's lines from view at the Carter house, but from Stiles's position they were plainly seen, formed apparently in double and triple lines of brigades, with artillery in the intervals between the columns. Hood had placed Cheatham's corps upon the Columbia turnpike with Cleburne's division on the east of the road, Brown's on the west of it, and Bate's in echelon on Brown's flank. Stewart's corps was on the right (east) of Cheatham, the order of his divisions from Cleburne's flank being French, Walthall, and Loring. Johnson's division was the only one of S. D. Lee's corps which had yet come up, and it was kept in reserve.

Very few battlefields of the war were so free from obstruction to the view. Here, along a mile and a half of front, the imposing array of the Confederate army could be seen advancing at quick step with trailed arms, the artillery in the intervals galloping forward, unlimbering and firing as soon as they were within range. A section of artillery with Wagner's brigades first opened on the advancing enemy, but as they approached it limbered up and deliberately trotted within the principal line, in accordance with orders sent it by the Chief of Artillery.

It was now four o'clock, and to the amazement of the thousands who were watching them, Wagner's infantry opened fire. There was a rattling fusillade for a few moments, Cleburne and Brown were checked for an instant, but the Confederate forces passed the flanks of Lane and Conrad, to right and left, a rush and a yell followed, and the two hapless brigades came streaming to the rear in a disorganized crowd, running rapidly to reach the parapets behind them. Orders were quickly sent down the line to withhold the fire at the centre till our own men should be in, but to make the utmost use of the artillery and small arms on the flanks. Opdycke was warned to be ready for a rush to the centre if the line should give way there, and the second line along the whole front was similarly prepared. A few moments later, the head of the flying mass was seen swarming over the works at the turnpike, and orders were sent for all reserves to charge. The men in the trenches, confused by the crowd trampling over them, and hearing Wagner's officers calling upon their men to rally at the rear, were carried away by the surging mass, and for the length of a regiment on the left, and more than that on the right, they fell away from the works. Neither Colonel White, commanding Reilly's second line, nor Colonel Opdycke waited for the word to charge, but were in motion before the order could reach them. White was nearest the parapet and reached it soonest, but his line did not reach quite to the turnpike. The Carter house and out-buildings on the right of the road obstructed the movement to the front, and Opdycke made part of his brigade oblique to the left till clear of the obstacles, and they then charged headlong upon the enemy. Part also went forward on the west of the houses, and Strickland's brigade rallying with them, the Confederates were driven back here also; but that the gap was open longer here than on the left, was proven by the enemy's dead who were found fifty yards within the lines.

David S. Stanley, U.S.A.

Stanley, forgetting his illness, had mounted his horse at the first sound of the cannonade, and the commandants of the two corps met on the turnpike just as Opdycke and his men were rushing to the front. Four guns, which had been placed a few yards to the left of the road, were in the enemy's hands, and were loaded with canister. These were turned upon the flank of Reilly's line, but the frightened horses had run off with the ammunition chests which contained the primers, and while the captors were unsuccessfully trying to fire the pieces, the reserve was upon them. Four other guns on the right of the road were also in the enemy's hands. There was a few minutes' fierce melée, but the guns were retaken and all of the men in gray who were inside the parapet were dead or prisoners. Yet the successive lines of assailants charging the works allowed no respite. Colonel White received a severe wound in the face, but refused to leave the line till after nightfall, and Opdycke had joined personally in the thickest of the deadly tussle on the turnpike. Our men, who had been driven back from the line, rallied by officers of all grades, returned to their posts, mingling with those who were there, making a wall three or four deep, those in rear loading the muskets for those who were firing. While rallying these men Stanley was wounded, his horse was shot under him, and he was reluctantly persuaded to return to his quarters for surgical help.

Farther to the right, and in part of what had been Strickland's brigade line, the Confederates of Brown's division held the outside of our parapet, so that when their comrades were driven back they were able to prevent our men from reaching it again. These, seizing upon fences and such material as came to hand, made a new barricade within about twenty-five yards of the first, and across the narrow interval the battle raged with most persistent fierceness. It was hard to tell where either brigade line ended, for Opdycke's men mingled with Reilly's on the one side, and with Strickland's on the other, and the three crowded the space where two had been. Officers and men had been conscious that with the centre broken, nothing but superhuman exertions could keep one wing, at least, of the little army from being driven into the river. They were equal to the occasion and they saved the day.

The railroad cut at Franklin, Tenn., where Union troops piled corpses.

But though the crisis of the engagement was at the centre, the fight was by no means all there. In other parts the veterans of the Atlanta campaign held their lines without flinching, though the assaults of Stewart's divisions rivalled those of Cheatham in their gallantry, and they made the most daring efforts to reach the bridges which were on that flank. Loring's men came upon the hedge in front of Stiles, and attempted in vain to tear it away, or to pass it. Henderson, who had been for some days ill, rejoined his brigade, and both he and Stiles directed the firing, which, sweeping along the ground, mowed down all before it. The Confederate officers urged their men to the right, hoping to pass through the railway cut, but here they were met by the shrapnel and canister of the guns in the fort north of the river. The batteries in Stiles's line were also admirably handled, and the attack here had never a chance.

On Casement's line, Walthall's and part of Loring's divisions made the assault, and as there was here no obstruction in front of the trench worth naming, the possibility of carrying such a line when properly held was fully tested. General John Adams led his brigade, riding straight at the ditch, leaping it, and mounting the parapet, where his horse was killed astride of it, and he himself pitched headlong among Casement's men, mortally wounded. Scott, commanding another of Loring's brigades, was wounded. In Walthall's division not only had Quarles fallen in leading his brigade to the assault, but the loss of officers was so great that, at the close of the battle, a captain was the ranking officer in that brigade. It was only when the last of Stewart's reserves had tried all that courage and dash could accomplish, that they relaxed their efforts. Some asked for quarter in the ditch, and came in as prisoners; some lay down in front of the hedge, and waited for darkness to enable them to crawl away undiscovered. The remainder fell back to a position near the extension of the line Wagner's brigades had occupied.

Nathan Kimball, U.S.A.

Cleburne had led his division forward, on the east of the central turnpike, with a desperation that was born of the wounded feelings he had shown in the morning, and he fell among the first who were at the ditch when the rush of our [Union] reserves restored the line between the cotton-gin and the road. His three successive lines pressed forward to avenge his death, but only to leave a thousand gallant officers and men beside him. On the other flank, Bate had moved forward his division at the same time with Brown, deploying as he went. His left reached beyond the Carter's Creek road as he neared the intrenchments, but the shape of our lines, which there bent back to the river, made him travel on a large curve, and his assault was considerably later than Brown's. It struck the right of Ruger's division, and the left of Kimball's, but finding the works before him stoutly held, and that the cavalry which he expected to advance upon his flank were not doing so, his attack was not pressed as determinedly as that of Brown. The success which this division seemed to have at the first, and the fact that for some distance they continued to hold the outside of the works, encouraged them to the most desperate and persistent efforts there.

General Strahl was with his brigade in the ditch, personally directing the fire of his men who got a foothold in the outside of the slope, and making those in [the] rear supply the front rank with loaded guns. As darkness came on, and it came quickly on that short winter day, the two breastworks, so little apart, were lines of continuous flame, as the men fired at the flash of each other's guns. On other parts of the field, there were, after dark, frequent volleys, as the Confederate generals strove to assist the central attack by strong demonstrations; but here the roar was for a long time incessant and deafening. Others suggested to Strahl to withdraw, or to surrender, but he steadily repeated the command, "keep firing," till he was himself struck down. He called for Colonel Stafford, to turn over the command, and they tried to carry him to the rear, but on the way a second and a third ball struck him, killing him instantly. Colonel Stafford continued the contest with the same determination. Messengers were sent to General Brown to tell him of Strahl's death and ask for orders, but they found that he was already disabled by a wound, and the staff supposed Strahl to be in command of the division. Cheatham had sent in all of Brown's brigades, but Gordon had been captured in the first melée, Gist, as well as Strahl, was dead, and Carter was wounded. Hood was called upon for assistance, and he sent forward Johnson's division of Lee's corps, but this, too, was driven back by that terrible fire, leaving General Manigault wounded on the field.

As a Confederate boy soldier, Sumner A. Cunningham was posted on the breastworks at Franklin. In the heat of the battle, as Gen. Strahl was passing him loaded guns, he asked, "What had we better do?" to which Strahl gave the famous reply: "Keep firing!" Moments later the general was shot down.

On the National [Union] side the One Hundred and Twelfth Illinois was brought over from Stiles's brigade, and put in to assist Strickland. An effort was made to get this regiment forward over the little interval between the two breastworks, but it was not successful. The oblique fire from our troops, on right and left, when they were not hotly engaged in front, was turned upon Cheatham's men, but it was nine o'clock before they gave up the contest, and those that were left were reformed on the line occupied by Stewart and Lee, though for more than an hour occasional volleys were exchanged.

At eleven o'clock, the whole front being quiet, Schofield ordered the withdrawal of our troops to the north side of the river, but an accidental fire broke out in the village, making a bright background on which our lines could be too plainly seen by the enemy, and it was necessary to wait an hour till the fire was extinguished. Kimball's division then marched by the rear to the wagon-bridge, Ruger's passed behind the lines to the railroad bridge,

Opdycke's brigade was sent to follow Kimball, and Reilly's division crossed behind Ruger, a line of skirmishers, under command of Major Dow, Inspector General, remaining in the trenches till all the rest were over and the plank taken from the wagon bridge, when these also crossed at the railway. The dead could not be removed, but the well disciplined ambulance corps, under Surgeon Frink, had taken off all the wounded who could endure transportation, except some who had crawled away into buildings and sheds and were not found in the darkness. Reilly's division carried off as trophies twenty-two battle flags of the enemy, and Opdycke's brigade ten.

The battle had been peculiar, partly by reason of the late hour in the day at which it began, which prolonged the hard fighting far into the night, and partly from the character of the weather. A day or two of sunshine had followed the continuous storms of the preceding fortnight, and the air had been still and hazy. The smoke of the battle did not rise or drift away, but settled on the field in a thick cloud, obscuring the vision far more than common. It was said that this had led to the mistake, on Hood's part, of supposing that his first advantage at the centre was much greater than in fact it was, and resulted in greater destruction to the Confederate troops, by repeated assaults after all real chance of success was gone.

The morning after the battle: "frozen" Confederate dead standing among the wounded.

The Confederate accounts of the condition of the field next morning are full of tragic interest. Before daybreak it was learned that the National lines were empty, and the plain was covered with torchbearers seeking their comrades and friends. Colonel Stafford was found in the ditch General Strahl and he had so stubbornly held. The dead lay literally in a pile about him. They had fallen about his legs and behind him, till when he at last received a fatal shot, he did not wholly fall, but was found stiffened in death and partly upright, seeming still to command the ghastly line of his comrades lying beneath the parapet. The color-bearer of the Forty-first Tennessee had fallen between the two lines of breastworks, but neither friend nor foe had been able to reach the flag till it was hidden by the night, and in the morning it was found where it dropped.

But even civil war rarely furnishes so sad a story as that which the [Confederate] Carter family have to tell. The house was occupied by an elderly man and his two daughters. Their presence during the day had been respected and had kept their property from unnecessary disturbance, and the day was so far gone that they thought there was no need to leave their home. The battle, when it came, broke upon them so suddenly that they did not dare to leave, and they took refuge in the cellar. The house was in the focus of the storm which raged about it for hours. They said that while the horrid din lasted, it seemed that they must die of terror if it did not cease; but when there was a lull, the suspense of fearful expectation seemed worse than the din, and it was almost a relief when the combat was renewed. The long night ended at last, and with the first light the young women found relief in ministering to the wounded who had crept into the house and outbuildings, and in carrying water to those on the field. But, as they climbed the parapet at the rear of the house, among the first they found was a young staff officer, their own brother [Theodrick "Tod" Carter], mortally wounded, lying, as he had fallen at sunset, almost at the door of his home.[51]

The withdrawal of Schofield's forces in the night left no opportunity to reckon the Confederate losses. Hood says that his casualties, computed ten days after the battle by means of the returns of "effective strength," were found to be 7,547 since the opening of this campaign, and including the losses about Columbia and Spring Hill. This, however, excludes all the slightly wounded who had returned to duty, and all officers, and makes no account of the accessions he had by the return of absentees and the joining of recruits. It still acknowledges a loss of 6,300 in this battle, of which 700 were prisoners in our hands. It is very certain that the

South view of the Carter House, Franklin, Tenn., circa 1904, "the very center of the battle."

whole Confederacy was deeply impressed with the frightful carnage of their troops, and their writers, with common accord, spoke of the desperate fighting as remarkable even in this war of desperate combats. The partial returns accessible seem to show clearly that no one of the divisions engaged (except Bate's), lost less than eight hundred, and that Brown's and Cleburne's, at the centre, and Loring's, on our left, lost much more heavily. The long list of general officers killed and wounded gives terrible significance to the recriminations which the affair at Spring Hill had excited. We have seen that Brown and all four of his brigadiers were disabled or killed. In Cleburne's division, Granbury besides himself fell. In Loring's division they lost Generals John Adams and Scott. In French's, Cockrell; in Walthall's, Quarles; and in Johnson's, Manigault; twelve generals in all, besides Stafford, and a long list of colonels and field officers who succeeded to brigade commands.

On the National [Union] side the losses were 2,326, of which more than one thousand were in the two brigades of Wagner, which were so unnecessarily compromised at the front. Near the centre, where the line was temporarily broken, the losses were naturally much heavier than on the flanks, where our men stoutly held the breastworks and fought under good cover. The result well illustrates the fearful odds at which the bravest troops assault a line of earthworks over open ground, even when a grave fault of a subordinate has given them an exceptional and unlooked-for advantage. General Wagner's place of duty was with the two brigades of his division which were exposed in front, and the order to bring them in without fighting had been sent through the Fourth Corps' head-quarters, and had been received by him. He was at the Carter house when the message came from the front that Hood was forming in line of battle, and, in a moment of excitement, forgetting himself and his orders, he sent back a command to fight. The overwhelming of the two brigades and the peril to the whole line were the necessary consequence. He rallied the disorganized brigades at the river, but they were not again carried into action.

During the battle and in preparation for any contingency which might arise, General Schofield directed General Wood to put the three brigades of his division in position to cover the flanks of the troops in front of the town, and to protect the bridges in case of need. Wood accordingly placed Post's brigade opposite Kimball's flank, below the town, Streight's near the bridges, and Beatty's above Fort Granger, all on the high ground of the north bank of the Harpeth; and these brigades maintained their position in the night till the rest of the infantry had passed through their lines and marched to Brentwood. General Wilson, with the cavalry, had, during the afternoon, a warm skirmish with Forrest, who tried in vain to cross the Harpeth beyond the left of Schofield's forces. Thomas sent a warm congratulatory despatch when the result of the engagement was announced to him; but, as he thought three days would still be needed to prepare his concentrated army for aggressive operations, and as this was a longer time than Schofield could engage to hold the line of the Harpeth without reinforcements, he directed the latter to retire upon Brentwood, and thence to Nashville. Despatches had been sent to General [Joseph A.] Cooper, who . . . had been stationed at Centreville, on Duck River, with a brigade of the Twenty-third Corps, directing him to fall back on Franklin. But unavoidable delays occurred, and when he approached Franklin, the enemy was in possession. He was similarly anticipated at Brentwood, but by coolness and good conduct brought in his command safely to Nashville.[52]
— UNION GENERAL JACOB DOLSON COX

Jacob D. Cox, U.S.A.

TRIBUTE TO HOOD BY A UNION VETERAN

☛ . . . I was somewhat surprised, and may say pained, during my recent trip South, to note the disposition among soldiers of the late Confederate Army to criticise and disparage the merits of Gen. Hood. That he made mistakes no unprejudiced student of the war between the States will deny, but that he was possessed of some of the best qualities that belong to great military commanders is equally indisputable.

As between the General and his critics touching the battle of Franklin, my sympathies are entirely with the former: while my admiration for the splendid valor exhibited by his heroic legions on that bloody field is not diminished by the fact that they were Americans all, and that today the [Confederate] survivors would fight as desperately for the "stars and stripes" as they did on that November day twenty-nine years ago for the "stars and bars." Franklin, from the Confederate standpoint of view, must ever remain one of the saddest tragedies of the civil war; on the other hand, there were in that battle possibilities to the Confederate cause [conservatism], and that came near being realized, scarcely second to those of any other in the great conflict. Had Hood won—and he came within an ace of it—and reaped the legitimate fruits of his victory, the verdict of history would have been reversed, and William Tecumseh Sherman, who took the flower of his army and with it made an unobstructed march to the sea, leaving but a remnant to contend against a foe that had taxed his every resource from Chattanooga to Atlanta, would have been hailed at the close as at the beginning of the war, "Crazy Sherman." No individual, not even Hood himself, had so much at stake in the fight at Franklin as the hero of the "march to the sea."[53] — UNION SOLDIER HONORABLE WASHINGTON GARDNER (Michigan)

Washington Gardner, U.S.A.

THE BATTLE AS VIEWED BY A YANKEE CLERGYMAN

☛ The night [of November 29, 1864, the day on which the Battle of Spring Hill was fought] seemed very long, but the tramp [northward toward Nashville] never ceased till the [Union] troops halted in the outskirts of Franklin. The advance arrived before daybreak, and the officers who led the way rode up to the Carter House (the first that they came to), and woke up the old man, the father of the Colonel, who showed us over the battlefield (who had been in the Confederate army, and was then at home on parole), and politely informed him that they would take possession of his house as their headquarters, to which, knowing the usages of war, he did not object.

. . . As they came up, they were turned to the right and left of the road, that the trains might pass through into the town. General Schofield at once pressed on to the river, where he had hoped to find the bridges standing, and pontoons, for which he had sent urgent messages to [Gen.] Thomas, ready to lay others, to pass over the artillery and baggage waggons. Instead of this, he found that the bridge connecting with the turnpike had been swept away, and that there was not a single pontoon with which to construct another. All that remained was the railroad bridge, which had to be planked to make it passable for waggons, and even then furnished but a slender resource for the passage of an army. Finding this condition, he returned to the front in a state of great anxiety. Thorough soldier as he was, he [Schofield] took the chances of war as they came, but for once he was taken aback at the unexpected position in which he was placed. "I never saw him," said General Cox, "so disturbed," as he now contemplated the probability, which a soldier dreads, of having to fight a battle with his back to a river, when a disaster is likely to prove fatal. (The orders of Hood were to "drive them into the river"!) But it was no time for idle regrets.

Gen. Cox was placed in command of the two divisions of the Twenty-third Corps, his own and Gen. Ruger's, and ordered to entrench strongly on a line running to the right and left of the turnpike. This was a new task for the soldiers, weary as they were with their all night's march, covering a distance of twenty-three miles. They were almost dead with fatigue, but not a moment was to be lost. As soon as they had snatched a hasty breakfast, they were set to work with spades and shovels, and in two or three hours had dug a ditch a mile and a half in length, throwing up the earth on the inside to make a breastwork (to which some added a log on the crest, raised three inches to leave space for their rifles), along which at intervals there were openings for the batteries; all which being done, they threw themselves upon the ground for a sleep which to many of them was to be their last.

Thomas H. Ruger, U.S.A.

General Schofield too was glad of a short interval of rest. For several days and nights he had had little sleep, except such as he got in the saddle. On the march he could clasp his hands round the pommel, and for a few minutes relapse into a state of forgetfulness, which, if not so refreshing as rest in a quiet bed or by the camp-fire, at least kept him from the point of utter exhaustion. So when the position had been made secure, he went to

the house of a good Union woman (it was pointed out to us as we rode through the street), and threw himself on a bed and fell asleep, and rested for an hour and a half, till he was awakened for orders.

All the forenoon the [Union] troops came pouring in, the last to arrive being those that had remained at Spring Hill. The Confederate army was but a few miles behind, sometimes approaching nearer, when the Federal rear-guard turned at bay, and showed such a grim front, with its batteries ranged so as to sweep the road, that its pursuers kept at a respectful distance. It was not till a few hours later that they were to come to close quarters. As the different divisions reached Franklin, there was another reversal of positions; for as those that arrived in the morning were now entrenched, they remained in their works; while the Fourth Corps under Gen. Stanley, which consisted of three divisions, was thus distributed: that of Kimball was placed at the extreme right of the line; that of Wagner was cut in two (two brigades being stationed outside of the works where they met a hard fate; while a third

The 1858 Franklin Courthouse as it looks today. During the battle it was used as headquarters by the Army of the Ohio; afterward it served as a hospital. (Photo Lochlainn Seabrook)

brigade, under Colonel Opdycke, was brought within the lines, and placed in the rear as a reserve; and, as we shall see, made one of the most brilliant charges of the day); while Wood's division marched through the town, and took its place on the other side of the river, where Stanley joined Schofield, and remained with him till the afternoon, as both fully expected that the attack of Hood's army would be aimed in that quarter rather than in front.

The disposition of the troops is indicated on the map of Franklin. . . . From this it will be seen that the position of the town is well fitted for defence, as it is surrounded on three sides by a river, and is open only on one. Across this open front, swelling out into a projecting curve, was drawn the line of [Union] entrenchments, to one end of which, near the railway, we had first driven to get a general view of the field. From that point we had pushed on two and a half miles out of town over the Columbia turnpike, till we came to where the road passes over high ground between two hills. Here, leaving our horses in charge of our black rider [that is, a Yankee slave], we ascended a hill on which were a few scattered trees, on the brow of which stood an old linden [tree], tall and gaunt, with its naked arms lifted against the sky. "Here," said Mr. [Sumner A.] Cunningham, "on the day of the battle, I saw General Hood ride forward alone on his horse, and halting near this tree, take out his field-glass, and gaze long and earnestly across the plain at the position of the enemy. All who were in sight of him watched him with eager eyes, for on the decision of that moment depended the fate of thousands. Presently he turned back to General Stewart, to whom I heard him say, 'We will make the fight!' and who received his extended hand with a sadness, which seemed to say, 'We may not meet again!' The die was cast. The order was instantly given to the [Confederate] troops, who, as they came over the hill, deployed, stretching out to the right and left, and forming in line of battle. On the opposite hill a military band had taken its position, and played some stirring Southern airs as the brave men marched down into the valley, which was to be to thousands of them the valley of death. The whole scene was the most thrilling that I ever saw in war."

The famous Linden tree on Winstead Hill where "the die was cast." It was here, prior to the battle, that Gen. Hood glassed the plain of Franklin. Then, turning to his men, he declared: "We will make the fight! We may not meet again!"

It was now the middle of the afternoon, and it took an hour for the army to defile into position. This hour, as may be supposed, was one of intense, though suppressed, excitement. We hear much of the noise of battle, but the stillness which precedes it is not less awful, as column after column, with measured step, takes its place in the ranks of death. It is the stillness which precedes the tempest, as thunder clouds gather darkly but silently. It is not till they touch each other that the storm bursts.

As the Confederate lines thus formed in front, General Hood rode forward to a hill, from which he could have a nearer view, so as to watch every movement, and be in position at once to receive reports and to give orders; while across the plain, on another hill overlooking the same scene, stood General Schofield, giving quick glances along his own lines, and away to the dark masses of men that were forming in mighty battalions for the death struggle.

It was now four o'clock, and as it was the last day of autumn,[54] and therefore one of the shortest days of the year, the sun was sinking in the west; but as the light struck across the plain, it shone on one of the most dazzling sights in the world—a great army drawn up in "Battle's magnificently stern array." These preparations were not unobserved. As it was an open plain between the two armies, every movement of the enemy was distinctly seen. Going to a projecting angle of the works, General Cox mounted the parapet, and with his field-glass took a long look at the large bodies of [Confederate] troops that were being massed at the foot of the hills; then mounting his horse, he rode to every point of the line, to see that all was ready for the attack. He had not long to wait, for already the troops were in motion. The day was nearly done, but enough remained to gain an immortal victory, and at that moment the dropping of a flag by General Cheatham gave the signal for the whole line to advance.

The battle began on the extreme left with a premature attack, which failed from its very precipitation. Gen. Bate (afterwards Governor of Tennessee, and now Senator) was a dashing soldier, and, being eager for the combat, pushed forward his division only to discover, as it came within range of the

William B. Bate, C.S.A.

enemy, that it was in advance of connecting lines. As his men looked to the right for a support, they saw that the other divisions were far behind; and as they had to take the whole fire, they retreated. Major [Joseph] Vaulx was an eye-witness of the attack and the repulse, and could not but regret, while he admired, the too impetuous valor of his brothers-in-arms.

But the fortune of war changed as the Confederates advanced in tremendous force, and it was now the turn of the Federals to experience a great disaster. In arranging the defences, two [Union] brigades had been placed outside of the town, across the turnpike, not as a position to be held, but simply to check and delay the attack. They were to fire a few rounds of artillery, and then to withdraw within the works and take their place in the line of defence, or to be held as a reserve. But as the approaching [Confederate] columns drew nearer, the [Union] officer in command, more brave than wise (who seems to have thought it the proper thing for a soldier to fight the enemy anywhere, and with any odds, even unsupported and alone), ordered his infantry to open fire, as if the battle were to be fought on that ground. The only explanation of his thus acting, not only without orders, but against orders, is that he "lost his head"—a very bad thing to lose in a battle. It were better that he had lost his life, for by this act of madness he lost a thousand men!

The result was what might have been expected. As the enemy's line of battle overlapped these brigades on both sides, it instantly closed in upon

them, and poured in such a fire that in a few moments they were utterly broken, and rushed at full speed back to the [Yankee] entrenchments, the Confederates following in hot pursuit. This was a double disaster. Not only were the brigades themselves overwhelmed, but the whole line had to hold its fire for fear of killing its own men; and so when the column rushed into the works, their pursuers rushed in after them, and were inside of the Federal lines, where they seized the shotted guns, and whirled them about to pour their contents into the flying crowd. But in the wild uproar, even the horses had caught the panic, and tearing away fled down the road, with the limbers containing the primers, so that the guns could not be discharged; and in the midst of this confusion, the tide of battle rolled back again, and all was recovered.

But this was not accomplished without a terrific conflict. In the rear of the line the ground descends in a gentle slope, and here a reserve brigade of two thousand men, under [Union] Colonel Opdycke, had been ordered to lie down, that they might not be exposed till they were needed. They had been warned of the danger of a break in the line, and now, at the call of their leader, they sprang to their feet, and rushed upon their assailants with the bayonet. So sudden was this apparition of armed men, starting up as if they had literally come out of the ground, and so tremendous their onset, that some accounts make their commander the hero of the battle. It would be more correct to say one of the heroes: for there is no need to exalt him at the expense of others, who shared in the same achievement. This brave officer now sleeps in a soldier's grave, and no praise can be too great for his

A. P. Baldwin, U.S.A.

courage at that decisive moment. But with his brigade were the portions of the two divisions under Reilly and Strickland that had been pushed back by the rush of Wagner's men, with the avalanche of Confederates behind; but who, as soon as the mingled mass swept by, so that they could distinguish friend from foe, reformed under those gallant soldiers.

All those [Union officers] in high command did their duty on this great day. General Stanley had been so sure that the attack of the enemy, when it came, would be on the other side of the river, where he was, that he had remained there with General Schofield till the firing began. Then he mounted his horse, and spurred to the front just in time to meet Wagner's brigades (that belonged to his own Fourth Corps) in full retreat; and exerted himself with the utmost energy to rally them, when his horse was shot under him, and he was wounded, and compelled, very much against his will, to return to his quarters for surgical skill. This threw the whole burden of command upon General Cox at a moment when the fate of the army was at stake. The imminent peril inspired him to increased activity, so that he seemed to fly from point to point. The voice of command could not be heard in the uproar of battle; but soldiers along the line could see that figure waving his sword in [the] air, and dashing wherever the combat was the deepest and the danger the greatest; and catching the inspiration, they reformed their broken ranks, and rushed upon the foe with a fury that was irresistible. The issue is briefly told: "There was a few minutes' fierce melée, but the guns were retaken, and all the men in gray inside the parapet were dead or prisoners."

Frank M. Cockrell, C.S.A.

General Schofield, who was watching the battle from the Fort, had felt his heart sink as he heard the yells with which the Confederates rushed over the works, and saw his own men swept away by the torrent. For the moment his heart stood still, for it seemed as if the battle was lost. But he soon breathed again, for though, at the distance he was, he could not see the forces engaged, since the roll of musketry was so incessant that friend and foe were wrapped in a dense cloud of smoke; yet, as the space behind was clear, and he could see that there were no more men running to the rear, he knew that his troops had regained their position.

This tremendous attack, which had threatened to destroy the Federal army, had been made in the centre by General Cheatham. Those who saw it coming say that never was there seen in war a grander sight than that of this whole Corps, massed in one mighty avalanche, sweeping down with a force that, it seemed, must be irresistible. One who looked at it with a soldier's eye, in which admiration mingled with dread, draws this picture: "The day had been bright and warm; the afternoon sun was setting on the distant hills; and in the hazy, yellow light, and with their yellowish-brown uniforms, those in the front ranks seemed to be magnified in size: one could almost imagine them to be phantoms sweeping along in the air. On they came, and in the centre their lines seemed to be many deep and unbroken, their red, tattered flags, as numerous as though every company bore them, flaring in the sun's rays, with conspicuous groups of general and staff officers in their midst, and a battery or two in splendid line charging along between the divisions."

This magnificence was terribly marred when the broken Federal line was restored, and the troops poured in their deadly fire. But still the charge was renewed with incredible fury. Again and again the Confederates rushed to the assault, even when it seemed hopeless, for the fire never slackened an instant. Instead of coming in fitful volleys, it was one continuous roar, sweeping away whole ranks of men; so that the survivors, as they staggered on, had to pass over the dying and the dead. [Confederate] Major Vaulx told us of the terrible slaughter in what passed under his own observation. He said: "Cheatham's old division (which still retained his name after he had been promoted to the command of a corps), was commanded by General John C. Brown. I was riding at his side when a ball struck him, and he fell forward on his horse's neck. I at once dismounted, and with others lifted him off and placed him in an ambulance, to be carried from the field, when I mounted and rode on, till of five general officers attached to our division, besides the commander, who had just been wounded, three were killed, and the fifth captured inside the Federal works; while of the staff officers attached to the division and to the four brigades, out of twelve, all but one were either killed or wounded! Such a loss of general and staff officers, I never saw before in any battle that I was in, and indeed do not think I ever read of in war."

While this murderous conflict was going on in the centre, another great [Confederate] Corps (that of Stewart), on the right of Cheatham, was converging towards the Federal lines. It came on with unbroken ranks till it got within range of the guns from the other side of the river, which swept that part of the field, and the heavy shot plunging into the solid columns, cut long lanes of death. But "officers on horseback and afoot were at every gap, trying to close them up," and the unfallen brave kept on till, as they came nearer and nearer the works, their numbers grew fewer. Never did men fight more desperately, and yet more hopelessly, as even Major Vaulx had to admit. To one who has shared in the fierce conflict of battle, it always seems as if there might have been done something more; and in the morning, as we were overlooking the field, and he recalled every feature of the great struggle, he had felt again all the excitement of the hour. Standing up in the carriage, and looking intently at the ground in front, along which Stewart's men had swept up to the Federal lines, he took in the whole scene, and it seemed as if a little more *elan*, or a thousand or two more men, might have carried the day, and he exclaimed, "By the Eternal! Stewart ought to have broken through!"

It was the natural feeling of a soldier, and yet in it he forgot that the Confederates, fearless as they were, were met with a courage equal to their

Joseph Vaulx, C.S.A.

own; and later in the day, when we [the Union] came to ride over the ground by which Stewart's Corps advanced, he saw at once the concentrated fire which it had to encounter, and was able to do more full justice to his brave companions-in-arms in recognizing that they had done all that human valor could do.

A gentleman recently living in New York, who was in command of a [Union] battery of steel guns, told me that as he moved forward, he passed over the hill on which General Hood had taken his position, in whose presence he suddenly found himself, and could not resist the impulse to pause a moment to see how a Commander looked in the midst of a battle. As he described the scene, "General Hood was sitting on a flat rock at the foot of a tree, his legs (one of which was of wood, to replace the original that had been lost in battle) extended in front, between which a fire had been lighted, and was still smouldering. At the instant one of General Cheatham's staff rode up in great excitement to report that he had carried a part of the Federal line, but could not hold it unless immediately reinforced. 'How does Gen. Cheatham estimate his loss?' asked Gen. Hood. 'At one-half of his whole command in killed and wounded,' was the reply. At this he raised his hands, clasping them together, and exclaimed 'O my God! This awful, awful day!'

John B. Hood, C.S.A.

Then recovering himself, he turned to one of his staff and said 'Go to Gen. Stephen D. Lee, and tell him to move up to the support of Gen. Cheatham, putting in Johnson's division first, and Clayton's next.' As my battery was between the two, I knew that my time had come, and moved on with the rest."

And now the battle raged all along the lines. The first success of the Confederates proved their ruin, as it had been so easily gained that it led them to repeat the attack, pouring division after division upon the works, only to see them melt away under that terrible fire. After these terrific charges, came what was not less impressive—the lulls of the battle.

First, there was a sound in the distance, as of a great multitude in motion, coupled with a fearful yell, which culminated in a rush and roar, as the living human wave struck upon the beach, and broke and rolled back again. Then for a few minutes there was a lull, as the enemy were gathering their forces to renew the onset—a comparative silence, broken only by the groans of the wounded and the dying. One who was in the battle writes me that the charge itself was not so dreadful as these moments of expectation.

Then rose the same terrific yell, and on they came again with the same desperate courage, but not with the same confidence: for they came, not with erect, martial air, but with heads bent low, as when facing a tempest, and caps drawn over their eyes, as if to shut from their sight the fate that awaited them.

At some points of the line the fire was such as no troops could stand long. Mr. Fullton, of the Maxwell House in Nashville, told me that he belonged to a troop of cavalry, which, when earthworks were to be attacked, were dismounted, every fourth man being detailed to hold the horses, while the rest served as infantry. As they advanced to the attack, they had hardly come within range before twelve of his company fell, and it seemed as if the whole would be swept away if they had not been ordered to throw themselves on the ground; and there, he said, "we lay the greater part of the night, not daring to raise our heads, nor to crawl forward even a few rods to give succor to the wounded and dying, whose groans we could hear distinctly right in front of us."

Alexander P. Stewart, C.S.A.

Driven back at one point, the [Confederate] charge was renewed at another with the same desperate courage, but always with the same result, until it was evident that further efforts were only a useless sacrifice of human life; and still the rage of battle was such that the attacks were repeated at intervals far into the night.

All these incidents of the day were [later] detailed to me with great minuteness, as we rode over that battle plain, by those who had been actors in the scenes they described. As we came back along the Columbia turnpike to the edge of the town, Mr. Carter met us and conducted us to the old Gin-House, which figures in all the accounts of the battle; and along the line of the entrenchments, pointing out where this or that Confederate division charged, and where the leaders fell. He had a theory of his own, according to which, if his plan had been followed, the result would have been otherwise. He was quite sure that if Gen. Bate, instead of rushing headlong into the fight, and getting severely crippled before the battle had really begun, had been a little less impetuous, and moved round farther to the left, he would have found the Federal line weaker, and might have made a charge that would have led to victory! Col. McEwen told how Forrest, the famous cavalry leader, went to Hood, and asked permission to cross the river with his mounted men, when, as he said, "he would flank the Federals out of their position in fifteen minutes!" But the Commander had made his own plan of battle; and being in an angry and imperious temper that day, was not in a mood to receive suggestions, or to listen to the proposal of any manoeuvre other than that of direct battle, and answered haughtily to the bold trooper who would flank the enemy, "No, no! Charge them out!"

But leaving speculations as to what might have been, we proceed to observe what actually took place. Mr. Carter now led the way to his house, which was the very centre of the battle. As it stands fronting on the Columbia turnpike, which runs through the town, and was but a few rods in the rear of the Federal breastworks, it was in the angle of two lines of battle: for, when the brigades of Wagner came flying in utter rout, they swept past its very door, followed by the Confederates, and the two sides fought around the dwelling; and when the onset was stayed, that portion of the line which was nearest was still held by the Confederates, while the Federals formed another line a few rods in the rear, so that the house was left between the two lines, and received the fire of both.

Corner of Columbia Avenue and Cleburne Street (not visible), Franklin, Tenn., the area where the "hottest" fighting took place. The cotton ginhouse was to the right (out of frame). The Carter House, which still stands, is located a few hundred yards up Columbia Ave. (straight ahead) on the left. (Photo Lochlainn Seabrook)

At this time the house contained a large family. The mother had died ten years before, but the father was still living, and with him were a son (who was now our guide,) and four daughters, a daughter-in-law, and several children. Of course, had they foreseen how near the battle would come to them, they would have fled to the other end of the town, or across the river. But in the early part of the day, while this was the headquarters there was perfect discipline, nobody was disturbed, and they felt that they were safest under their own roof. And when at last the storm came, it burst upon them so suddenly that it was too late to escape. There was only one spot of safety, the cellar, and there they all took refuge.

Here, self-imprisoned, they could not see what was going on about them, but they heard the roar above their heads, for the thunderings and lightnings were incessant. As the mass of soldiers surged round the dwelling, some who shrank from the awful fire crowded into the cellar way, when the family retreated behind a partition, but as there was no means of barring the door, the intruders pressed in there also, and into a third underground refuge, when, as Mr. Carter himself tells the tale, he "turned upon them and cursed them and drove them out!" But even in this dark hiding-place, he could look through the grated window, and ask the "Yankee soldiers" how the battle was going!

After a time the fury of the battle abated, for the first shock, which was the most tremendous of all, had spent itself in an hour. Then darkness came, so that the opposing lines were partly hidden from each other. But still they fought on, even when they could see to fire only by the flashing of each other's guns.

As we came up from the cellar, and went round the house, we saw that its southern side, which was exposed to the Confederate fire, was riddled with shot, as were all the outbuildings having the same exposure. How deadly it proved was shown by the fact that Mr. Carter counted fifty-seven dead, besides the wounded, in his door-yard the next morning.

Leading the way across the garden, my friend Cunningham stopped under a pear-tree, which recalled the memory of that fearful night. It was in the line of the earthworks thrown up by the Union soldiers, outside of which was a ditch. Of this part of the line the Confederates had got possession, and held it; but so terrible was the fire that again and again the parapet was swept of the heads that rose above it. The trench below

The tiny 1817 McPhail-Cliffe Office, Franklin, Tenn., was used as part of Gen. Schofield's Union headquarters on the morning of November 30, 1864. (Photo Lochlainn Seabrook)

was filled with the dying and the dead. Standing with one foot on the bodies of his fallen comrades, and the other on the bank, he rested his gun—a short Enfield rifle that he had been permitted to carry, as he was so young and small—on the top of the works. The line had been so thinned out that only a solitary fellow-soldier stood near him, and now he was shot, and fell heavily (he was a large man) against him, and tumbled over into the mass of dead below. Thus left alone, he asked General Strahl, who had stood for a long while in the trench, and passed up loaded guns to men posted on the embankment, "What had we better do?" The answer was "Keep firing!" But Strahl himself was soon shot, and while being carried to the rear, was struck again and instantly killed. He was succeeded by Colonel Stafford, who also was killed, and sank in such a position that he was braced up by the mass of bodies around him, so that when the morning came, he was standing there

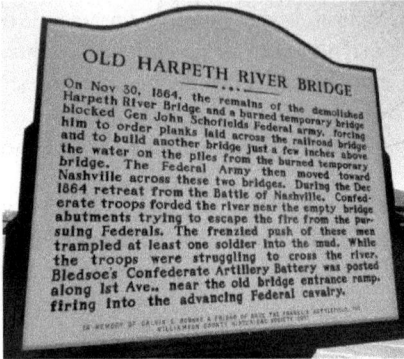

Historical marker at the site of the Old Harpeth River Bridge, Franklin, Tenn. (Photo Lochlainn Seabrook)

stark and cold, as if still ready to give command to the army of the dead!

These were ghastly memories to come back after the lapse of so many years. How changed the scene now! It was the month of March, and already the breath of Spring was in the air, and the little pear-tree, which had lived through all the storm and tempest of that fearful night, though scarred in many places, yet had healed its wounds, and was putting forth its leaves fresh and green, as if it had never heard the sound of battle. So, while men die, the life of nature keeps on, and even draws nourishment from their blood.

[Back to the battle:] . . . About half past ten o'clock Gen. Schofield sent orders to Gen. Cox that at midnight the troops should be withdrawn—an order which the latter received with great pain, as he felt that there was now an opportunity to destroy Hood's army. The [Confederate] prisoners who had been taken, or who had come in and given themselves up, reported that they were all cut to pieces; that regiments and divisions were left almost without officers; and that the whole army was utterly demoralized. These reports were confirmed by the heaps of [Confederate] dead that lay all along the line. Seeing and hearing this, Cox felt that there was an opportunity such as seldom occurs in war, to end the campaign with a single blow, and he implored Gen. Schofield to remain, saying in the ardor of his confidence that he "would answer with his head" for the result of the next day. The answer of Schofield was all that could gratify the pride of a soldier. He said: "Tell Gen. Cox he has won a glorious victory, and I have no doubt we could do as he suggests in the morning. But my orders from Gen. Thomas are imperative, and we must move back to Nashville as soon as possible."

So the order was reluctantly issued, and at midnight the troops were ready to move. But at this moment a fire broke out in the town—a building had perhaps been set on fire for the purpose—which cast a light over the place so as to expose every movement to the

Remnants of the Old Harpeth River Bridge, Franklin, Tenn. (Photo Lochlainn Seabrook)

enemy. This caused a delay, but at length the fires sank down in their ashes, and the wearied soldiers once more strung their knapsacks on their backs. The trains had been already got across the river, and the broken columns resumed their march.

Ignorant of all this, Hood, who was brooding gloomily over the events of the day had called a council of war at midnight, at which the commanders of the three corps, Cheatham, Stewart, and Lee, reported their several commands as half destroyed. As he listened to tale after tale of disaster, his temper, soured before, became almost savage. Still he bore up with an unconquered mind; and, even while one-fourth of his army were stretched in their blood upon the ground, he declared that he would renew the contest the next morning. One thing he had to give him confidence. His heavy artillery, of which he had felt the want the day before, was now coming up, and he said he "would open the battle with a hundred guns!" Indeed he could not wait for the break of day, but at three o'clock startled the town with a tremendous roar. Said Col. McEwen, "I thought it would take my head off." But to his amazement there was no reply, for the Federal army was across the river, and on its way to Nashville, and only heard in the distance these last thunders of impotent rage and fury. The sound did not hasten their steps an instant,

Hood tried to renew the battle on the morning of December 1, 1864, but, unbeknownst to him, "the Federal army was [already] across the river, and on its way to Nashville." Assuming he had forced the Yankee retreat, he at first designated Franklin a Confederate victory.

nor evoke a taunt or a cheer. Still they plodded on silent as the stars that were shining above them. In that long procession there was none of the pomp and circumstance of war, nothing of that which might be expected in an army a few hours after a great victory. . . . As there was no shout of triumph for the living, there was no mourning for the dead. "Not a drum was heard nor a funeral note." The [Yankee] soldiers were weary and worn: many of them had been wounded; some had their heads bound up; others carried their arms in slings; some, leaning on their comrades, dragged themselves slowly along. Sadder than all, as they took their places in the ranks, they missed many from their side: comrades that but a few hours ago were "full of lusty life," were now lying in their new made graves, or unburied on the plain.

An army thus stricken, was in no mood for exultation. What a contrast was this night march to that of the night before! Only twenty-four hours had passed, but in that time they had lived years! Thus blood-stained with the wounds of battle, yet victorious, in the gray of morning they found rest in the camps round the city of Nashville.

This [Union] withdrawal had been wholly voluntary, yet Hood had the weakness to telegraph to Richmond, "We attacked the enemy at Franklin, and drove him from his outer line of temporary works into his interior line, which he abandoned during the night, and rapidly retreated to Nashville!" as if he had gained a victory. But this pretence deceived no one, for it was impossible to hide from his own soldiers the awful carnage of that day.

As soon as daylight made it visible, they had before their eyes the horrors of the battlefield, on which lay six thousand dead and wounded! Though used to war, they had never seen such a sight before. There were places where the dead lay one upon another, five deep; while for some distance the ground was covered. A Confederate officer tells me that the next morning he mounted his horse to ride to the front, but as he drew near the horse started back, affrighted at the smell of blood, and at the human figures that stared at him from the ground, with every look of agony in their

At the time of the Battle of Franklin, Columbia Pike (upon which both armies traveled) was a single lane dirt road, as can be seen in this photo from around 35 years later. The photographer is looking north toward Franklin, with Winstead Hill on the left and Breezy Hill on the right. Both prominences played a role in the bloody conflict that took place here November 30, 1864.

faces; and he dismounted and endeavored to pick his way on foot, but so thick were the slain that he said, "I do not think it extravagant to say that for two hundred yards from the line of the intrenchments, I could have walked on the dead, stepping from one body to another!" . . . Hardly less striking than this were the groups scattered far and wide over the field: for the dead lay in heaps, torn to pieces by shot and shell, till they had almost lost the semblance of humanity; with the brave creatures that had carried them into the battle stretched beside them. . . .

In the presence of such awful misery, it seems an unworthy intrusion of human pride to dispute the honors of the day. It is not an hour to boast when thousands of our fellow-beings are lying on the ground in the agonies of death. The object for which the battle was fought—to destroy the Union army—had utterly failed, and so far it was a Union victory. But if only the glory be considered, there is glory enough for all: for never was there a more splendid display of courage and devotion, than in the Confederates who that day sacrificed their lives in vain.[55] — REVEREND HENRY MARTYN FIELD (Massachusetts)

UNION OFFICER WRITES TO WIDOW OF GEN. JOHN ADAMS

☛ October 25, 1891 - Dear Madam: I am in receipt of your very kind letter of the 21st, inst., and hasten to reply. . . . I have often since the great battle of Franklin asked myself the questions, Who was [Confederate] Gen. Adams? Has he a wife and children? And if so, how much would they give to know just how he died and all the facts as I know them? . . .

The battle of Franklin was one of the most desperate contests of the war. I was in command of the skirmish line of Cox's Division. Gen. Adams's and Gen. Brown's Brigades, of the Confederate army, were massed in front of our division. We had during the forenoon thrown up breastworks of earth some ten feet thick and five feet high, behind which our men stood protected; while the enemy came up in an open field and charged upon us. They had no protection, and were mowed down like grass before the scythe. This will explain to you how desperate was the undertaking to dislodge our army from behind this impenetrable breastwork and the sublime heroism of the men who undertook the perilous task and almost succeeded.

The Confederates came on with bayonets fixed and moving at a steady walk. My skirmishers, who were stationed some hundred yards in front of our breastworks, were brushed out of the way and rapidly fell back to the main line. By this time the enemy was within a few paces and received a terrific volley from our guns. They fell by thousands, and their decimated ranks fell back to reform and come again. In this way nine separate and distinct charges were made, each time men falling in every direction and each time being repulsed. I doubt that if in the history of the world a single instance of such desperate and undaunted valor can be produced.

James H. Wilson, U.S.A.

In one of these charges, more desperate than any that followed, Gen. Adams rode up to our works and, cheering his men, made an attempt to leap his horse over them. The horse fell dead upon the top of the embankment and the General was caught under him, pierced with bullets. As soon as the charge was repulsed our men sprang upon the works and lifted the horse, while others dragged the General from under him. He was perfectly conscious, and knew his fate. He asked for water, as all dying men do in battle as the lifeblood drips from the body. One of my men gave him a canteen of water, while another brought an armload of cotton from an old gin near by and made him a pillow. The General gallantly thanked them, and, in answer to our expressions of sorrow at his sad fate, he said, "It is the fate of a soldier to die for his country," and expired.

Robert Baker, one of my men, took the saddle from the dead horse and threw it in [Union] Gen. Casement's ambulance, who expressed it to his

home in Ohio. Some three years ago I received a letter from Gen.
Casement, in which he wrote me that he had the saddle labeled and carefully
laid away as a trophy of the war. I write a letter to-day to the General,
asking him to send the saddle to me, that I may forward it to you. I am also
glad to know that you recovered the General's watch, chain, and ring, and
will say that if your sons—who, you inform me, are connected with the
Missouri Pacific Railway—should have business on this branch of the road,
I would be glad to have them call at my office. Mr. Wilder, the agent here,
knows me, and would no doubt bring them. I hope that my imperfect
description may be of some interest to you.[56] — UNION LIEUT.-COL.
EDWARD ADAMS BAKER (65th Indiana Infantry)

FROM THE "OTHER SIDE" AT FRANKLIN

☛ I have read . . . [the Confederate] experiences in
the battle of Franklin, 1864, and . . . [write], as near
as I can remember, the position of our division,
engaged in that battle; also my own experiences.

At four o'clock A.M., November 30, by direction
of Gen. Stanley, the division took up the line of march
en route from Columbia to Franklin, as the rear guard
of the army. The Second and Third Brigades of the
Fourth Corps were to march in parallel along the
road. Col. Opdycke to move in line of battle in the
rear. The enemy began skirmishing with Col.
Opdycke early in the morning.

Joseph Conrad, U.S.A.

When the division reached Winstead's Hill, two miles south of
Franklin, Gen. Stanley gave the order to halt, in order to allow us to get
breakfast. Col. Opdycke's brigade was placed in the gap and on the point
east of the pike, with a section of artillery, to check the advance of the
enemy, who was pursuing us at the time. Col. Lane's Brigade was placed
in position on Col. Opdycke's left; Col. Conrad went into line on the left
of Col. Lane; Gen. Whitaker's Brigade, of the First Division, occupied the
heights on the right of the pike. The enemy soon appeared, with a heavy
force, and the command was put under arms to be ready to repel an attack.

Quickly after these dispositions were made. I observed the troops of
the corps moving toward Franklin, and the command withdrew from its
advanced position on the heights and followed on toward town. When
within half a mile of town, we received orders to reoccupy the heights and
to hold them as long as we could.

It was not long before the enemy was moving two heavy columns of
infantry against our lines, one by each of the pikes leading into Franklin, one
column turning our left flank. We then withdrew and joined the main line
of our troops, which surrounded the town. Lane's Brigade and a section of

artillery took position on the hills to the right of the pike, about one mile north of Winstead's Hill. He remained skirmishing till his right flank was about to be turned, when he was ordered to leave a heavy line of skirmishers to hold the hill as long as possible, and to withdraw his brigade and take position on the right of the Third Brigade, which had been formed on the left of the pike, about four hundred yards in advance of our main line, at the same time placing a section of artillery on the pike between these two brigades. The commanders of the Second and Third Brigades were ordered to hold their positions long enough to develop the force of the enemy, but not to attempt to fight if threatened by the enemy in force.

Opdycke's Brigade was destined to have a new experience, that of defending the breastworks against assault. We had assaulted works and had helped build them by the mile, but had never yet had the opportunity to defend one against serious assault. The assault at Franklin was made by two infantry corps and one division of a third corps—forty thousand men. A more determined and persistent effort to carry a position was never made in this or any other war. At the first onset the assaulting troops carried the works at the center; while Opdycke's Brigade charged in the breach, retook the works after a fierce struggle, and held them. Right here was the worst fighting I ever experienced in my life. Many of the enemy

The McGavock Confederate Cemetery, Franklin, Tenn., where nearly 1,500 Confederate soldiers rest in eternal peace. (Photo Lochlainn Seabrook)

were killed inside our lines. The fighting lasted until near midnight, when we abandoned our works and crossed the river, leaving our dead and wounded, losing a great many men through capture. Never did men fight more gallantly.

I was in the front line on that charge, and I never saw the dead lie so thick as I saw them that night—a ghastly sight in the white starlight. It is doubtful if in any battle of modern times there were as many personal encounters as occurred at Franklin. I myself was clubbed over the head with a musket held by a six-foot "Johnny," and I saw all kinds of stars for a minute or two. At midnight we started for Nashville.

I would like to hear from any ex-Confederate who was in that battle. I kept a diary while in the service, and, looking it over sometimes, I wonder how I ever managed to get home alive.[57] — UNION SOLDIER E. R. DALY (Elyria, Ohio)

The historic district of Franklin, Tenn., still looks much like it did in 1864. (Photo Lochlainn Seabrook)

Street signs at the corner of Columbia Avenue and Confederate Drive, Franklin, Tenn., memorializing the Southern patriots who fought here November 30, 1864. (Photo Lochlainn Seabrook)

Carter House, parlor, first floor, as it appeared in 1971. The Carter family, and neighbors, hid in the house's cellar during the Battle of Franklin.

Carnton Plantation, Franklin, Tenn., used as a Confederate field hospital during and after the Battle of Franklin. (Photo Lochlainn Seabrook)

City signage on Hillsboro Road, at the northwest entrance to Franklin, Tenn. (Photo Lochlainn Seabrook)

Cultural signage, Franklin, Tenn. (Photo Lochlainn Seabrook)

APPENDIX A

ADDRESS AT THE FRANKLIN, TENNESSEE, CONFEDERATE MONUMENT DEDICATION

NOVEMBER 30, 1899

The occasion which brings you here is one to which we have all looked forward with interest. We are making history to-day. *Future generations will point back with pride to this day—that their fathers and mothers, thirty-five years after the close of one of the bloodiest wars of history, when all passion had subsided, all animosities had been buried, and all sections of our common country were at peace with each other as brothers, had paid this tribute of affection to the memory of their countrymen.* A generation has passed, and this is in part the work of a new generation. *The corner stone of this monument is love—every rock in its foundation is cemented in love; every stroke of the chisel that worked out its beautiful symmetry was made in love; love, pure and simple, welled up in grateful hearts, as a token of which we transmit this monument to posterity.*

This is the work of the noble women of Williamson County. They are the daughters of those women who near forty years ago gave such impetus to the cause of the Confederacy. Go back in memory to the stirring days of 1861. The women were as active as the men. There was an invading army at our borders; nothing was left to be done but go. The women aroused an enthusiasm that brooked no opposition, and *be it said to the lasting credit of Williamson [County, Tenn.] that she put more men in the field than she had voters.* The wife to her husband, the mother to her boy, the sister to her brother, the maiden to her sweetheart—all said: "Go. God be with you till we meet again! Should the fate of war befall you, and should that banner around which cluster the bright hopes of the Confederacy go down, you shall ever live in the hearts of your countrymen." We saw them go. They were boys, the flower of the land. Amid the hardships and deprivations of camp life, the desolation of the battlefield, they knew that promise would be redeemed, and gathered strength and courage from the fact. That promise has been as sacred with the daughters as it was with the mothers.

Who first suggested this monument, and that it be placed on the public square? is a question that has been asked. No man or woman can claim the credit. *The sentiment that something should be done to show to coming ages that we who saw and knew the Confederate soldier honored and loved him was spontaneous, and had its origin in no*

Celebrated Confederate soldier, nicknamed "Chip" (due to the missing piece in the brim of his hat), atop the Confederate monument, Franklin, Tennessee. (Photo Lochlainn Seabrook)

single mind; and upon the idea that a monument to his memory was the proper means we were all unanimous.

Some at first preferred the beautiful McGavock [Confederate] Cemetery, the gift of that venerable gentleman [the owner John W. McGavock] whose memory is lovingly cherished by every man, woman, and child in Williamson County. The locality, while sacred as the resting place of the hallowed bones of our heroes, was too far removed from daily public contact.

Some preferred the battlefield, in sight of the railroad, that strangers in passing might know that we honor our countrymen. But *we don't build it for strangers; we build it for our children. We teach our children patriotism, to love, honor, and defend the government under which we live; and in recent months children of Confederate soldiers, who revere the government, offered the opportunity, have proven themselves to be worthy sons of honored sires.* And all, with rare exceptions, gradually came to the conclusion that the public square was the place, *that our children might know by daily observation of this monument that their fathers and mothers regarded the Confederate soldier as the grandest character in all history.*

History has her heroes from the earliest age. They stand out upon her pages as beacon lights, and have ignited the chivalry in the soul of many a boy. But we did not see them; we read about them. The men who left their homes that they had not seen for four years and followed [Confederate Gen. John Bell] Hood out of Tennessee, when they so plainly saw that the star of the Confederacy had begun to set, were heroes before whom, in our eyes, all others pale into comparative insignificance. The men who followed Lee from Richmond, when they could but see that his Appomattox was near, were men in whose fidelity and valor the gods delight. These men were Southerners, our own countrymen. Some of them were from Williamson County. Some of them are here to-day; some have passed over the river,

Franklin Square and the town's beautiful Confederate monument, as they appeared in 1909.

and are resting under the shades of eternity, awaiting the coming of their comrades, which will be short. *These Confederate Veterans are the men we desire to honor. It is an honor to belong to the race that could produce them. Our children should know them, and the richest heritage we have to leave them is that their blood flows through their veins. Such is the sentiment that built this monument and located it where it is.*

Contrast for a moment their home-coming in 1865 with that of their sons [from the Spanish-American War] in 1899—you have just witnessed the latter, in the sentiment of which we all heartily join. Ragged, foot-sore, weary, desolation on all sides, burned cities and homes, wasted fields. There was no trumpet to herald their coming; the sound of their approaching footsteps wasted away in the surrounding stillness. . . . But their countrymen and their countrywomen gave them a greeting worth more than the evanescent, fickle "*Io triumphe*" of the returning conqueror. With a silent, melancholy joy you met them; with outstretched arms and hearts full of love you received them, and showed to them then, as you have shown to the world for the thirty-five years since then, that you were proud of the record they made.

Only a few words in regard to the manner in which the money was raised. It is the work of the women of Williamson County. They have commanded the willing services of the men, and we have come and gone at their bidding. The monument fund was started by a few women about fourteen years ago, and their number was continually increased. By ice cream suppers, concerts, cake walks, etc., from time to time a few dollars were raised. During this period these women devoted much of their attention to raising funds for needy Confederate soldiers, for the Soldiers' Home, McGavock Cemetery, etc. On this account the completion of the monument was deferred, and not for lack of interest in it. They succeeded in raising nearly $500. In 1896 Chapter No. 14. United Daughters of the Confederacy, was organized at Franklin, of which the most of these women became members. The chapter took charge of the enterprise, and went to work with a determination that saw nothing but success, and you see the result. While our pride in our soldiers is great, it is not greater than that we have in these women. *All praise to the United Daughters of the Confederacy! All praise to the women of Williamson County! It took just such women as we have to make the Confederate soldier what he was.*

Donations have come to them from all sources. Democrats, Republicans, Populists, Prohibitionists, vied with each other in their contributions. School children gave their dimes. *Federal soldiers took stock, and this is the gift of all conditions of life, to stand as a monument of the affection of a grateful people.* While many Confederate soldiers have been liberal in their donations, I for one, have thought that we should not require much of them, because this is done not by them, but for them; it is done in their honor.

J. H. Henderson.

While history for a season may be colored by the conquerors, and thus shadow the truth, in time it will right itself, and the world will know, as we now know, that no age or country has ever produced the superior of our countrymen in courage, fidelity, and nobleness of character, and we wish to offer for coming generations our humble testimony of these virtues.

A monument in honor of the Confederate soldier, or something that will impress my children with the grandeur of his character, has been the burden of my heart ever since I have had children. Now that it is an accomplished fact, no man can be more rejoiced.

On the fateful field of Franklin, in addition to the great fatality in the ranks, there was unprecedented fatality among the officers. They led their men. Six generals, one major general, and five brigadiers dead upon the field, and as many wounded. [Patrick Ronayne] Cleburne, [John] Adams, [John Carpenter] Carter, [Hiram Bronson] Granbury, [States Rights] Gist, and [Otho French] Strahl—*names that will ever be sacred to Southerners, as brave and as heroic as any in all the annals of history*.[58] — J. H. HENDERSON

APPENDIX B

ADDRESS AT FRANKLIN, TENNESSEE, DECORATION OF CONFEDERATE GRAVES AT MCGAVOCK CONFEDERATE CEMETERY

CIRCA 1901

Ladies, Gentlemen, Comrades, Daughters and Sons of the Soldiers of the South, we have met here to-day to reverence and honor our departed heroes, who have passed over the river, and are resting under the shade of the trees, waiting for us.

We have met not only to cherish their memories, but to vindicate their characters and the purity of their motives. *In 1861 the Southern people were the best informed, the most energetic, the most religious, and the most democratic people upon the earth.*

The McGavock Confederate Cemetery, Franklin, Tenn., established by John and Carrie McGavock of Carnton Plantation. The author, who is related to the McGavocks, has numerous cousins buried here. (Photo Lochlainn Seabrook)

And I can also truthfully state that the people of the South were more attached to the Union as it existed under the Constitution than were the people of the North. We were learned in agriculture, law, medicine, the literature of the Jews, Greeks, Romans, French, and English, and surpassed all others in statecraft. Our young men would gladly listen for hours to the discussion of political questions.

Our institution of slavery had partly separated us from other nations. *The Southern people were mostly descended from the soldiers of the revolution. Almost every Southern soldier could remember that his ancestors fought in the war of the revolution [1775], the war of 1812, the Indian wars [1812-1821], or the war with Mexico [1846-1848]. We had devised, framed, and fashioned the Union, and added to it all of its grandeur and glory. We had extended its boundaries from Virginia to California, and hence were attached to it.*

The young people may ask: Why did these heroes who sleep in their graves before us willingly offer up their lives? Why did they seek to dissolve the Union they had loved so much? The whole story can be told in a few minutes: As we understood it in 1861, and as our departed comrades understood it, with their parting words they urged us to be true and faithful.

When we gained our independence [from Britain in 1776] we were thirteen separate and distinct colonies. A more perfect Union was formed. The Constitution was the written contract entered into. The first trouble came during the war of 1812, when *the North*, in convention [of Liberals] at Hartford, Conn., *asserted the right of secession, and threatened to withdraw from the Union,* and make an ignoble peace with England. The next trouble came when Congress imposed a tariff for the declared purpose of protecting the manufactories of the North. John C. Calhoun requested that the acknowledged purpose be expressed in the act; so that its constitutionality could be tested in the Supreme Court of the United States. When this was refused he asserted that there was a tribunal of last resort—the people of the States. This was called "Nullification." *The North was the first to assert the right of secession; the South first to assert the right of nullification. Our rights in slaves were declared protected by the Constitution, the acts of Congress, and the decision of the Supreme Court of the United States. The North became "nullifiers," and a majority of the [Liberal] Northern States, through their Legislatures, nullified the Constitution, the acts of Congress, and the decision of the Supreme Court, and became the advocates of nullification.* In the midst of these disagreements, secret societies in the North collected, armed, and equipped a band of [Left-wing] men, who, with John Brown as their leader, invaded Virginia. These men were captured, convicted, and executed. Though they were guilty of treason and murder, the North threatened the South with vengeance for executing the law. *The Republican [then the Liberal party] or abolition party had been teaching the doctrine of secession and nullification, and had been vigorously enforcing the doctrine of nullification; but when it elected a President, the whole tone of the party changed.*

The [Conservative] South having been driven in desperation to resort to secession, the abolition party of the North became at once a great Union party. Their [Liberal] President, Mr. Lincoln, was a wise, shrewd, and cunning politician, with many virtues. Under his lead his party was taught that henceforth nothing but the preservation of the Union was to be taught and urged. He at once pacified the Democratic party of the North by bestowing offices and declaring that he sought nothing but the preservation of the Union. He raised a great army, but this army was not

John McGavock.

to turn its arms against the nullifiers of the North, but the secessionists of the South. The South remembered the John Brown raid and his intention as expressed in his code of laws, and *it was the universal opinion of the South that the raid of John Brown was but the advance guard of the Northern armies.* And thus this great war was begun. No power upon the earth could prevent it. No individual should be held responsible for what happened. Grim-visaged war ruled supreme. *We would have the young of this age and future ages understand what we thought and how we felt. How could we trust the promises of the [Liberal] North as long as their acts of nullification remained upon their statute books? How could we trust them when they raised armies to coerce us into obedience, and openly refused themselves to be bound by the Constitution, the acts of Congress, and the opinion of the Supreme Court?*

We did not fully understand what the negroes would do, or how they would act. *The North had brought them from Africa in their ships, and had sold them in the South, and now proposed to release them and place them in power over the white people of the South. This must have been prompted by the blindest prejudice and a most malignant heart or ignorance of the true philosophy of the situation. The South had done more for the negro than all the North put together. We had civilized and Christianized 4,000,000 of that race. Be it said to the honor of the women of the South: They had looked after the physical and spiritual welfare of the negro, and had so Christianized him and so attached him to his home that he was true and faithful in the hour of our greatest need, and many anticipated evils [such as slave uprisings and riots] did not come.*

To fully understand the Southern soldier, we must look at these things as we understood them in 1861. The North placed 2,500,000 soldiers in the field. The largest, the best-equipped and best-disciplined army of modern times; perhaps the world had never before seen such an army. This army was composed in part of the flower of the North, and all Europe was open to draw upon for soldiers, money, and all the sinews of war. The South had only 600,000 soldiers, no ships or arms, no money, and no friends. But we continued the unequal contest for four long years under countless disadvantages and deprivations.

There were no classes in the South; all white men were free and equal. In that grand army of the South the farmer, the planter, the mechanic, the merchant, the rich and the poor stood side by side upon terms of perfect equality—one in love and friendship. The boy of seventeen stood shoulder to shoulder with the man of sixty, and the boy was required to assume the responsibilities and perform the duties of a man. If those who sleep before us could come from their graves and appear before us as they appeared upon this bloody battlefield, you would be amazed at the great number of boys from seventeen to twenty years of age.

The brave never die in vain. The courage of the South had much to do with the preservation of local self-government [that is, states' rights] and the individual rights of man [that is, constitutionalism] . Happy must be the souls of our departed comrades who died for what has been called the "lost cause" when they look down upon us and see that, by wisdom, courage, patience, endurance, and devotion to law and order, we have gained the victory, and to know that *the whole civilized world gives more honor and praise to the vanquished than to the victors.*[59]

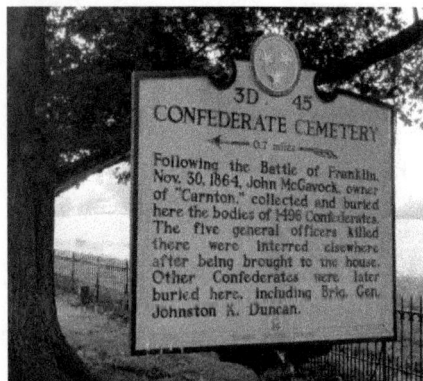

Historical marker, McGavock Confederate Cemetery, Franklin, Tenn. Established in 1866, it is the only privately owned Confederate cemetery in the U.S. (Photo Lochlainn Seabrook)

We stand among the graves of our departed comrades who gave their lives for their country [at the Battle of Franklin II] on the 30th day of November, 1864. They come from all the States of our dear and beautiful South, and now rest with us. Some had come from Germany, Scotland, and Ireland to make their homes in the South. *They have erected their own monuments, more durable than marble or brass. They have made their names immortal.* We will decorate their graves. Upon one we will place the corn flower in honor of the place of his birth among the vine-clad hills of the Rhine, and with it we will place the magnolia in memory of the State of his adoption. Upon some we will place the lily, and upon some the shamrock, and upon all the beautiful and fragrant flowers of the South. You Daughters of the South will care for their graves, and will *cherish their virtues and deeds in your hearts forever.* Let us not forget to ever bear in kindly and honorable remembrance that peerless Southern gentleman, Col. John McGavock, now departed, and his noble wife (Caroline), who so generously gave this resting place for our dead in this most beautiful spot.[60] — JUDGE H. H. COOK

APPENDIX C

A CONFEDERATE GIRL'S EXPERIENCE
INSIDE THE LINES AT FRANKLIN

1895

I was a pupil in the old Franklin Female Institute—the alma mater of so many brilliant, women, the mothers and grandmothers of the present generation. Nashville owes a debt of gratitude to at least two of its graduates, Misses Fannie and Martha O'Bryan.

At the time of these reminiscences, Miss Walker (now Mrs. J. P. Hanner), was the principal. The pupils numbered about 175, and as wide awake set of Southern girls as could be found.

While we were trying to concentrate our minds on our books one ear was always open to the varied sounds of the life and the rattle of drums, the clatter of horses' hoofs, and the electrifying notes of the bugle. We were allowed always to run to the front gate to see soldiers pass. If they were "our boys," we waved our bonnets and handkerchiefs—if they were yankees, and we watched Buell's army of thousands pass, we looked and felt dismayed.

On an ever memorable day, the 30th of November, [1864,] we assembled at school as usual. Our teachers' faces looked unusually serious that morning. The Federal couriers were dashing hither and thither. The officers were gathering in squads, and the cavalry, with swords and sabres clanking, were driving their spurs into their horses' flanks and galloping out to first one picket post and then another on the roads leading south and southwest of town. The bell called us in the chapel. We were told to take our books and go home, as there was every indication that we would be in the midst of a battle that day.

At four o'clock that afternoon I stood in our front door and heard musketry in the neighborhood of Col. Carter's on the Columbia pike. To this day I can recall the feeling of sickening dread that came over me. As the evening wore on, the firing became more frequent, and nearer and louder; then the cannon began to roar from the fort.

My father realizing that we were in range of the guns from both armies told us to run down into the cellar. We hastily threw a change of clothing into a bundle and obeyed at once. My mother, who never knew what fear meant in her life, was a little reluctant to go and leave the upper part of the house to the tender mercies of soldiers, but she finally joined us in the basement. A few minutes later there was a crash! and down came a deluge of dust and gravel. The usually placid face of our old black mammy, now thoroughly frightened, appeared on the scene. She said a cannon ball had torn a hole in the side of the meat house and broken her wash kettle to pieces. She left the supper on the stove and fled precipitately into the cellar.

After that, the only way we could get anything to eat was by sending a guard, who was in the yard, to the kitchen after it. The patter of the bullets on the blinds was anything but soothing. The incessant booming of cannon and the rattle of the guns continued until midnight, then the firing gradually ceased; we, of course, were in ignorance of who was in possession of the place, but all the while hoping and praying that it might be our boys.

About one o'clock we thought the town was being reduced to ashes, but it turned out to be the burning of the Odd Fellows Hall on the square. About four o'clock we heard the tramping of feet and the sound of voices. Our hearts jumped into our mouths, and what joy when we learned that our own soldiers were in possession of the town! We first learned it from the men who carried Col. Sam Shannon, who had been wounded, to his sister's house, our next door neighbor. Our men were in possession of the town! We didn't "stand on ceremonies" getting out of the cellar. Our doors were thrown wide open, and in a few minutes a big fire was burning in the parlor. The first man to enter was Gen. Wm. Bate, all bespattered with mud and blackened with powder, but a grand and glorious soldier under it all. I will not attempt to picture the meeting between him and my father, who had been a life-long friend. Next came Gen. Tom Benton Smith, with the impersonation of a chivalric, gallant soldier, wearing under the mud and dirt his recent hard-earned honors. Poor fellow, how short lived were his joys! A cruel [Yankee] sabre cut at Nashville forever dethroned his reason, and he is now in a Tennessee Asylum for the insane.

Space fails me to mention the long list of friends who came that day and received our warmest welcome. I shall mention what a reproof my sisters received from some of their soldier sweethearts. An uncle of ours, who made his home in New York city, during the previous summer had my sisters to visit him, and, of course, they replenished their wardrobes while there. On the morning after the battle they wanted to compliment their soldier friends by "looking their best," so they put on their prettiest dresses. The soldiers were so unaccustomed to seeing stylish new dresses, that they actually doubted their loyalty, thought they should have on homespun dresses instead of "store clothes."

In the afternoon, December 1ˢᵗ, some of us went to the battlefield, to give water and wine to the wounded. All of us carried cups from which to refresh the thirsty. Horrors! what sights that met our girlish eyes! The dead and wounded lined the Columbia pike for the distance of a mile. In Mrs. Sykes' yard, Gen. Hood sat talking with some of his staff officers. I didn't look upon him as a hero, because nothing had been accomplished that could benefit us.

As we approached Col. Carter's house, we could scarcely walk without stepping on dead or dying men. We could hear the cries of the wounded, of which Col. Carter's house was full to overflowing. As I entered the front door, I heard a poor fellow giving his sympathetic comrades a dying message for his loved ones at home. We went through the hall, and were shown into a little room where a soft light revealed all that was mortal of the gifted young genius, Theo ["Tod"] Carter, who under the pseudonym of "Mint Julep," wrote such delightful letters to the *Chattanooga Rebel*. Bending over him, begging for just one word of recognition, was his faithful and heartbroken sister. The night before the battle he had taken supper at Mr. Green Neely's (the father of our postmaster), and was in a perfect ecstacy of joy at the thought of seeing his family on the morrow, from whom he had been separated so long. But alas! when the morrow came, that active, brilliant brain had been pierced by one of the enemy's bullets; he was carried home and ministered to by those faithful sisters, and died, I think, without ever having spoken a word.

From this sad scene, we passed on to a locust thicket, and men in every conceivable position could be seen, some with their fingers on the triggers, and death struck them so suddenly they didn't move. Past the thicket we saw trenches dug to receive as many as ten bodies. On the left of the pike, around the old gin house, men and horses were lying so thick that we could not walk. Gen. Adam's horse was lying stark and stiff upon the breastworks. Ambulances were being filled with the wounded as fast as possible, and the whole town was turned into a hospital.

Instead of saying lessons at school the day after the battle, I watched the wounded men being carried in.

Our house was full as could be; from morning until night we made bandages and scraped linen lint with which to dress the wounds, besides making jellies and soups with which to nourish them.

The times were not without their romances. Only a short time afterward a handsome young Missouri surgeon, in charge of one of the hospitals, married one of our most prominent young ladies. Another Missourian, who was wounded here, and was so popular with the girls, married also. A young soldier who was an artist, met on the field one of our young ladies, who was also of an artistic turn of mind, and the year following they were married.[61]

— FRANCES, "A SCHOOL GIRL OF 1864"

APPENDIX D

A SOUTHERN WOMAN'S PERSPECTIVE
1890

Let us examine . . . the narrative of General Hood's movements after the evacuation of Atlanta. In reviewing these forces on the 18th of September [1864] President Davis had told Cheatham's Division to be of good cheer, for within a short while their faces would be turned homeward, and their feet pressing Tennessee soil.

Ten days later General Hood took up his line of march toward Tennessee, with Sherman following on the 3rd of October. On the 12th the Confederates took Dalton; thence they proceeded to La Fayette; and from that place they moved across to Gadsden, Ala., pursued by General Sherman as far as Gaylesville. The latter cut himself loose from all communication with the North, and took up his celebrated movement to the sea, while General Hood advanced into Tennessee, driving the enemy constantly before him, and forcing General Schofield to fall back from Columbia on the 26th of November, with the loss of a large quantity of stores.

[According to one Confederate narrator:] "The retreat to Franklin was one of constant fighting. Skirmishing of the very heaviest and deadliest character was maintained all the way. Forrest hung like a raging tiger upon the [Union] rear. . . . The Confederates pressed on—Forrest leading, Stewart next, and Cheatham following. Lee was still in the rear, but coming up. The enemy were closely pushed, retreated rapidly, and left evidences of their haste on every side."

In this way the march was continued until on the evening of November 30, when General Hood found himself before the frowning breastworks of the town of Franklin.

The troops under him were now upon the soil of their native State, which had long been in the possession of the enemy. They could look around them and see the homes that had been denied them for many a long day, and for which now at their very thresholds they were to do battle. With such incentives as these urging them to action, at five o'clock in the afternoon they began one of the grandest attacks of the war, an attack illuminated by as sublime an exhibition of personal courage from [Confederate] field-officer to the humblest private in the ranks as has ever blazoned the records of human bravery.

In the face of a fire that tore ghastly gashes in their unfaltering column they stormed and drove the enemy from the first line of works. Onward they advanced, stopping not nor halting however obstinately the enemy might resist and however thick might be that awful, bloody field of carnage with their own dead. On that crimson battle-ground many a knightly soul went out while within sight of the firesides where their wives and little ones were praying and watching for the absent soldiers' return.

This was the last battle of gallant Pat Cleburne, "the bravest of the brave." The gallant Gist fell in this conflict, as also did Brown, Strahl, Johnson, and Manigault; and though the gray dawn of the next day saw the Federal army shattered and flying toward Nashville, the victory had been dearly bought, and the sacrifice that these Tennesseans offered upon the altars of their country was great.

General Hood followed the enemy to Nashville, and on the 2nd of December proceeded to invest the city, where General Thomas was strongly fortified with a largely superior force.[62] — ANN E. SNYDER (Nashville, Tenn.)

NOTES

1. Woods, p. 47.

2. On Lincoln's socialistic, Marxist, and communist thoughts, ideas, and tendencies, see my books: 1) *Lincoln's War: The Real Cause, The Real Winner, the Real Loser*; 2) *Abraham Lincoln Was a Liberal, Jefferson Davis Was a Conservative: The Missing Key to Understanding the American Civil War*; 3) *Abraham Lincoln: The Southern View*. Also see McCarty, passim; Browder, passim; Benson and Kennedy, passim.

3. See J. W. Jones, TDMV, pp. 144, 200-201, 273.

4. See Seabrook, TAHSR, passim. See also, Pollard, LC, p. 178; J. H. Franklin, pp. 101, 111, 130, 149; Nicolay and Hay, ALCW, Vol. 1, p. 627.

5. BISG (the "Book Industry Study Group"), for example—a Left-wing organization which describes itself as "the leading book trade association for standardized best practices, research and information, and events"—gives its BISAC ("Book Industry Standards and Communications") listing for works on the War for Southern Independence under the heading "Civil War Period, 1850-1877." Nearly all books published in the U.S.A. today are under the categorizational control of this progressive group located in New York City.

6. See e.g., Seabrook, TQJD, pp. 30, 38, 76.

7. See e.g., J. Davis, RFCG, Vol. 1, pp. 55, 422; Vol. 2, pp. 4, 161, 454, 610. Besides using the term "Civil War" himself, President Davis cites numerous other individuals who use it as well.

8. See e.g., *Confederate Veteran*, March 1912, p. 122.

9. Minutes of the Eighth Annual Meeting, July 1898, p. 87.

10. For more on the nihilistic, atheistic, anti-life, anti-tradition, anti-American, anti-Constitution, anti-capitalism, anti-South agenda of the Victorian Republican Party (then the Liberal Party) and the modern Democrat Party (now the Liberal Party), otherwise known as "The Communist/Socialist Rules for Revolution," see Hasselberg, pp. 2350-2351; Lenin, passim; Marx and Engels, passim; B. Dodd, passim.

11. *Confederate Veteran*, July 1901, p. 318.

12. Seabrook, EOTBOF, p. 11.

13. For more on these topics, see Seabrook, EYWTAASIW.

14. For a detailed discussion of this topic, see Seabrook, ALWALJDWAC.

15. For more on what is known as "Cleburne's Memorial" emancipation plan, see Seabrook, EYWTAASIW.

16. Hood, pp. 292-300. Note: The title of this entry is my own. L.S.

17. Evans, Vol. 8, pp. 154-161. Note: The title of this entry is my own. L.S.

18. For more on this topic, see Seabrook, AWAITBLA.

19. For more on this topic, as well as related topics, see Seabrook, TGYC.

20. For more on this topic, see Seabrook, LW.

21. *Confederate Veteran*, January 1900, pp. 6-10. Notes: 1) Gen. Brown was commander-in-chief of the United Confederate Veterans (UCV) from 1890 to 1904 (the year of his death). The UCV is now the Sons of Confederate Veterans (SCV), an organization to which I belong. 2) The title of this entry is my own. L.S.

22. *Confederate Veteran*, May 1904, p. 227.

23. *Confederate Veteran*, November 1896, p. 388.

24. For a detailed look at the McGavocks and Carnton Plantation, see Seabrook, TMOCP; Seabrook, CPGS.

25. *Confederate Veteran*, June 1897, p. 299.

26. *Confederate Veteran*, June 1897, p. 302.

27. Contrary to popular misconception (both North and South), the Southern Cause was not "lost." For an in-depth discussion of this topic, see Seabrook, LW.

28. Watkins, pp. 208-212. Note: The title of this entry is my own, derived from Watkins' comments. L.S.

29. *Confederate Veteran*, January 1893, pp. 16, 31. (See also *Confederate Veteran*, April 1893, pp. 101-102.) Notes: 1) Cunningham was the founder of *Confederate Veteran* magazine in 1893, and served as its editor until his death in 1913. 2) The title of this entry is my own. L.S.

30. *Confederate Veteran*, November 1893, p. 339.

31. For a detailed look at the McGavocks and Carnton Plantation, see Seabrook, TMOCP; Seabrook, CPGS.

32. *Confederate Veteran*, December 1897, p. 600.

33. For a detailed look at the McGavocks and Carnton Plantation, see Seabrook, TMOCP; Seabrook, CPGS.

34. *Confederate Veteran*, January 1898, p. 13. Note: The title of this entry is my own. L.S.

35. *Confederate Veteran*, January 1898, p. 27.

36. *Confederate Veteran*, March 1901, pp. 116-117. Note: The title of this entry is my own. L.S.

37. The original source material for this particular paragraph contained numerous lacunae, which I took the liberty of correcting according to my knowledge of this incident.

38. *Confederate Veteran*, May 1901, p. 221. Notes: 1) The next day, December 1, from Hood on down, many Confederate soldiers at first assumed that they had won Franklin due to the fact that the Union soldiers had already abandoned the town and were headed north toward Nashville, even leaving their dead upon the field in their rush to "retreat." Yankee veterans, of course, later scoffed at this assertion, claiming that their march to Nashville would have occurred no matter what took place at Franklin, that the battle there had never been intended to begin with, and that they were the victors, not the Confederates. This topic continues to be debated to this day. 2) The title of this entry is my own. L.S.

39. *Confederate Veteran*, July 1901, p. 314. Note: The title of this entry is my own. L.S.

40. *Confederate Veteran*, October 1902, pp. 457-458. Note: The title of this entry is my own. L.S.

41. *Confederate Veteran*, October 1902, p. 458. Note: The title of this entry is my own. L.S.

42. *Confederate Veteran*, November 1902, pp. 500-502. Notes: 1) Some sources spell George's surname Leavell. 2) The title of this entry is my own. L.S.

43. *Confederate Veteran*, June 1894, p. 186. Note: The title of this entry is my own. L.S.

44. *Confederate Veteran*, December 1922, p. 448.

45. For a detailed look at the McGavocks and Carnton Plantation, see Seabrook, TMOCP; Seabrook, CPGS.

46. Seabrook, TMOCP, pp. 372-373 (2011 paperback edition). See also *Confederate Veteran*, December 1922, p. 448. Note: The title of this entry is my own. L.S.

47. *Confederate Veteran*, September 1895, p. 274.

48. This was the Confederates' great "lost opportunity" at Spring Hill. For a detailed discussion of this conflict, see Seabrook, TBOSH.

49. It is revealing that the Yankee writer seems to consider Southerners who shot "rebels after the war was over" a sign of "loyalty" to the U.S. government. Had he any understanding of the origins of the Southern Confederacy, or even the history of our country, he could not have made such a statement. In any event, here in Dixie, Southerners who detest their own region and prefer Yankee ways (e.g., Liberal politics), are still referred to disparagingly as "scallywags," just as they were during the War for Southern Independence.

50. Scofield, pp. 21-46. Note: The title of this entry is my own. L.S.

51. For more on Tod and the Carter family of Franklin, Tenn., see Seabrook, TMOCP; Seabrook, EOTBOF.

52. Cox, pp. 82-98. Note: The title of this entry is my own. L.S.

53. *Confederate Veteran*, December 1893, p. 375.

54. Technically speaking, in the year 1864 Autumn did not end until the first day of the Winter Solstice, three weeks later, on December 21. L.S.

55. Field, pp. 227-256. Notes: 1) The title of this entry is my own. 2) Field, though he was not a soldier in the War and was thus not present at Franklin, often uses the first person as if he was. This form of story telling is acceptable, particularly from one (a Yankee) who supported his region's cause; that is, liberalism. 3) To tell his story Field uses the accounts of both Union and Confederate soldiers who were at Franklin. This makes his description historically valuable, which is why I have included it. 4) Field's comments are particularly important and interesting in that they come from a civilian and a clergyman. 5) The problem with Rev. Field is that, like all Liberals today (and indeed, many Conservatives as well) he has a complete misunderstanding of the reasons for the War and the actual causes for which each side fought, so his comments must be read with this fact in mind. Yet, even through the nescience of others, much can be learned. L.S.

56. *Confederate Veteran*, June 1897, pp. 300-301. Note: The title of this entry is my own. L.S.

57. *Confederate Veteran*, February 1899, p. 59.

58. Seabrook, CM, pp. 382-386. My emphasis.

59. There was no "lost cause." Learn the full story of the War for Southern Independence in my book, *Lincoln's War: The Real Cause, the Real Winner, the Real Loser*.

60. Seabrook, CM, pp. 388-392. My emphasis. For more on the McGavock Confederate Cemetery, including a complete list of the Confederate dead buried there, see Seabrook, EOTBOF; Seabrook, CPGS.

61. *Confederate Veteran*, March 1895, pp. 72-73.

62. Snyder, pp. 228-230. Notes: 1) For more on the Battle of Nashville, see Seabrook, TBON. 2) The title of this entry is my own. L.S.

BIBLIOGRAPHY

And Suggested Reading

Abbot, Willis John. *Battlefields and Campfires: A Narrative of the Principle Military Operations of the Civil War*. New York, NY: Dodd, Mead and Co., 1890.

Ashe, Captain Samuel A'Court. *A Southern View of the Invasion of the Southern States and War of 1861-1865*. 1935. Crawfordville, GA: Ruffin Flag Co., 1938 ed.

Benson, Al, Jr., and Walter Donald Kennedy. *Lincoln's Marxists*. Gretna, LA: Pelican, 2011.

Boyd, James P. *Parties, Problems, and Leaders of 1896: An Impartial Presentation of Living National Questions*. Chicago, IL: Publishers' Union, 1896.

Brock, Robert Alonzo (ed.). *Southern Historical Society Papers*. 52 vols. Richmond, VA: Southern Historical Society, 1876-1943.

Browder, Earl. *Lincoln and the Communists*. New York, NY: Workers Library Publishers, Inc., 1936.

Bryan, William Jennings. *The First Battle: A Story of the Campaign of 1896*. Chicago, IL: W. B. Conkey Co., 1896.

Burgess, John William. *The Civil War and the Constitution, 1859-1865*. 2 vols. New York, NY: Charles Scribner's Sons, 1910.

Burns, James MacGregor. *The Vineyard of Liberty*. New York, NY: Alfred A. Knopf, 1982.

Campaigns in Kentucky and Tennessee, Including the Battle of Chickamauga, 1862-1864. Papers of the Military Historical Society of Massachusetts, Vol. 7. Boston, MA: The Military Historical Society of Massachusetts, 1908.

Christian, George Llewellyn. *Abraham Lincoln: An Address Delivered Before R. E. Lee Camp, No. 1 Confederate Veterans at Richmond, VA, October 29, 1909*. Richmond, VA: L. H. Jenkins, 1909.

——. *A Capitol Disaster: A Chapter of Reconstruction in Virginia*. Richmond, VA: self-published, 1915.

——. *Confederate Memories and Experiences*. Richmond, VA: self-published, 1915.

Clare, Israel Smith. *Illustrated History of All Nations*. 15 vols. New York, NY: The Christian Herald, 1909.

Collins, R. M. *Chapters From the Unwritten History of the War Between the States; or, The Incidents in the Life of a Confederate Soldier in Camp, on the March, in the Great Battles, and in Prison*. St. Louis, MO: self-published, 1893.

Confederate Memorial Literary Society. *Catalogue of the Confederate Museum, of the Confederate Memorial Literary Society, Corner Twelfth and Clay Streets, Richmond, Virginia*. Richmond, VA: self-published, 1905.

Confederate Veteran (Sumner Archibald Cunningham, ed.). 40 vols. Nashville, TN: Confederate Veteran, 1893-1932.

Cox, Jacob Dolson. *The March to the Sea: Franklin and Nashville*. New York, NY: Charles Scribner's Sons, 1882.

Cunningham, Sumner Archibald. *Reminiscences of the Forty-first Tennessee Regiment*. Shelbyville, TN: self-published, 1867.

Davis, Jefferson. *The Rise and Fall of the Confederate Government*. 2 vols. New York, NY: D. Appleton and Co., 1881.

Dodd, Bella. *School of Darkness*. New York, NY: P. J. Kennedy and Sons, 1954.

Dodge, Grenville M. *The Battle of Atlanta and Other Campaigns, Addresses, Etc.* Council Bluffs, IA: self-published, 1910.

Evans, Clement Anselm (ed.). *Confederate Military History*. 12 vols. Atlanta, GA: Confederate Publishing Co., 1899.

Field, Henry Martyn. *Bright Skies and Dark Shadows*. New York, NY: Charles Scribner's Sons, 1890.

Fiske, John. *The Mississippi Valley in the Civil War*. Cambridge, MA: Houghton, Mifflin and Co., 1902.

Franklin, John Hope. *Reconstruction After the Civil War*. Chicago, IL: University of Chicago Press, 1961.

Hasselberg, P. D. (ed.). *Parliamentary Debates: First Session, Fortieth Parliament, 1982, House of Representatives* (Vol. 445). Wellington, New Zealand: Government Printer, 1982.

Hood, John Bell. *Advance and Retreat: Personal Experiences in the United States and Confederate Armies*. New

Orleans, LA: G. T. Beauregard, 1880.

Johnson, Richard W. *Memoir of Maj.-Gen. George H. Thomas.* Philadelphia, PA: J. B. Lippincott and Co., 1881.

Johnson, Robert Underwood, and Clarence Clough Buel (eds.). *Battles and Leaders of the Civil War.* 4 vols. New York, NY: The Century Co., 1884-1888.

Johnstone, Huger William. *Truth of War Conspiracy, 1861.* Idylwild, GA: H. W. Johnstone, 1921.

Jones, John William. *The Davis Memorial Volume; Or Our Dead President, Jefferson Davis and the World's Tribute to His Memory.* Richmond, VA: B. F. Johnson, 1889.

La Bree, Ben (ed.). *The Confederate Soldier in the Civil War, 1861-1865.* Louisville, KY: Prentice Press, 1897.

Lenin, Vladimir. *"Left Wing" Communism: An Infantile Disorder.* Detroit, MI: The Marxian Educational Society, 1921.

Livermore, Thomas L. *Numbers and Losses in the Civil War in America, 1861-65.* 1900. Carlisle, PA: John Kallmann, 1996 ed.

Magliocca, Gerard N. *The Tragedy of William Jennings Bryan: Constitutional Law and the Politics of Backlash.* New Haven, CT: Yale University Press, 2011.

Marx, Karl, and Frederick Engels. *Manifesto of the Communist Party.* Chicago, IL: Charles H. Kerr and Co., 1906.

McCarty, Burke (ed.). *Little Sermons in Socialism by Abraham Lincoln.* Chicago, IL: The Chicago Daily Socialist, 1910.

McMurray, William Josiah. *History of the Twentieth Tennessee Regiment Volunteer Infantry, C.S.A.* Nashville, TN: The Publication Committee, 1904.

McPherson, James M. *Abraham Lincoln and the Second American Revolution.* New York, NY: Oxford University Press, 1991.

Meriwether, Elizabeth Avery (pseudonym, "George Edmonds"). *Facts and Falsehoods Concerning the War on the South, 1861-1865.* Memphis, TN: A. R. Taylor and Co., 1904.

Miller, Francis Trevelyan, and Robert S. Lanier (eds.). *The Photographic History of the Civil War.* 10 vols. New York, NY: The Review of Reviews Co., 1911.

Minutes of the Eighth Annual Meeting and Reunion of the United Confederate Veterans, Atlanta, GA, July 20-23, 1898. New Orleans, LA: United Confederate Veterans, 1907.

Minutes of the Ninth Annual Meeting and Reunion of the United Confederate Veterans, Charleston, SC, May 10-13, 1899. New Orleans, LA: United Confederate Veterans, 1907.

Minutes of the Twelfth Annual Meeting and Reunion of the United Confederate Veterans, Dallas, TX, April 22-25, 1902. New Orleans, LA: United Confederate Veterans, 1907.

Muzzey, David Saville. *The United States of America: Vol. 1, To the Civil War.* Boston, MA: Ginn and Co., 1922.

——. *The American Adventure: Vol. 2, From the Civil War.* 1924. New York, NY: Harper and Brothers, 1927 ed.

Nicolay, John G., and John Hay (eds.). *Abraham Lincoln: A History.* 10 vols. New York, NY: The Century Co., 1890.

——. *Complete Works of Abraham Lincoln.* 12 vols. 1894. New York, NY: Francis D. Tandy Co., 1905 ed.

——. *Abraham Lincoln: Complete Works.* 12 vols. 1894. New York, NY: The Century Co., 1907 ed.

ORA (full title: *The War of the Rebellion: A Compilation of the Official Records of the Union and Confederate Armies*). 70 vols. Washington, DC: Government Printing Office, 1880.

ORN (full title: *Official Records of the Union and Confederate Navies in the War of the Rebellion*). 30 vols. Washington, DC: Government Printing Office, 1894.

Pollard, Edward Alfred. *The Lost Cause.* New York, NY: E. B. Treat and Co., 1867.

Richardson, John Anderson. *Richardson's Defense of the South.* Atlanta, GA: A. B. Caldwell, 1914.

Rogers, William P. *The Three Secession Movements in the United States: Samuel J. Tilden, the Democratic Candidate for Presidency; the Advisor, Aider and Abettor of the Great Secession Movement of 1860; and One of the Authors of the Infamous Resolution of 1864; His Claims as a Statesman and Reformer Considered.* Boston, MA: John Wilson and Son, 1876.

Rove, Karl. *The Triumph of William McKinley: Why the Election of 1896 Still Matters.* New York, NY: Simon and Schuster, 2015.

Rutherford, Mildred Lewis. *Truths of History: A Fair, Unbiased, Impartial, Unprejudiced and Conscientious Study of History.* Athens, GA: n.p., 1920.

Scofield, Levi T. *The Retreat From Pulaski to Nashville, Tenn.: Battle of Franklin, Tennessee, November 30th, 1864.* Cleveland, OH: Press of the Caxton Co., 1909.

Seabrook, Lochlainn. *Carnton Plantation Ghost Stories: True Tales of the Unexplained from Tennessee's Most Haunted Civil War House!* 2005. Franklin, TN, 2016 ed.

———. *Nathan Bedford Forrest: Southern Hero, American Patriot.* 2007. Franklin, TN, 2010 ed.

———. *Abraham Lincoln: The Southern View.* 2007. Franklin, TN: Sea Raven Press, 2013 ed.

———. *The McGavocks of Carnton Plantation: A Southern History - Celebrating One of Dixie's Most Noble Confederate Families and Their Tennessee Home.* 2008. Franklin, TN, 2011ed.

———. *A Rebel Born: A Defense of Nathan Bedford Forrest.* 2010. Franklin, TN: Sea Raven Press, 2011 ed.

———. *A Rebel Born: The Screenplay* (for the film). 2011. Franklin, TN: Sea Raven Press.

———. *Everything You Were Taught About the Civil War is Wrong, Ask a Southerner!* 2010. Franklin, TN: Sea Raven Press, revised 2014 ed.

———. *The Quotable Jefferson Davis: Selections From the Writings and Speeches of the Confederacy's First President.* Franklin, TN: Sea Raven Press, 2011.

———. *The Quotable Robert E. Lee: Selections From the Writings and Speeches of the South's Most Beloved Civil War General.* Franklin, TN: Sea Raven Press, 2011 Sesquicentennial Civil War Edition.

———. *Lincolnology: The Real Abraham Lincoln Revealed In His Own Words.* Franklin, TN: Sea Raven Press, 2011.

———. *The Unquotable Abraham Lincoln: The President's Quotes They Don't Want You To Know!* Franklin, TN: Sea Raven Press, 2011.

———. *Honest Jeff and Dishonest Abe: A Southern Children's Guide to the Civil War.* Franklin, TN: Sea Raven Press, 2012.

———. *Encyclopedia of the Battle of Franklin - A Comprehensive Guide to the Conflict that Changed the Civil War.* Franklin, TN: Sea Raven Press, 2012.

———. *The Quotable Nathan Bedford Forrest: Selections From the Writings and Speeches of the Confederacy's Most Brilliant Cavalryman.* Spring Hill, TN: Sea Raven Press, 2012.

———. *Forrest! 99 Reasons to Love Nathan Bedford Forrest.* Spring Hill, TN: Sea Raven Press, 2012.

———. *Give 'Em Hell Boys! The Complete Military Correspondence of Nathan Bedford Forrest.* Spring Hill, TN: Sea Raven Press, 2012.

———. *The Constitution of the Confederate States of America Explained: A Clause-by-Clause Study of the South's Magna Carta.* Spring Hill, TN: Sea Raven Press, 2012 Sesquicentennial Civil War Edition.

———. *The Great Impersonator: 99 Reasons to Dislike Abraham Lincoln.* Spring Hill, TN: Sea Raven Press, 2012.

———. *The Old Rebel: Robert E. Lee As He Was Seen By His Contemporaries.* Spring Hill, TN: Sea Raven Press, 2012 Sesquicentennial Civil War Edition.

———. *The Quotable Stonewall Jackson: Selections From the Writings and Speeches of the South's Most Famous General.* Spring Hill, TN: Sea Raven Press, 2012 Sesquicentennial Civil War Edition.

———. *Saddle, Sword, and Gun: A Biography of Nathan Bedford Forrest for Teens.* Spring Hill, TN: Sea Raven Press, 2013.

———. *The Alexander H. Stephens Reader: Excerpts From the Works of a Confederate Founding Father.* Spring Hill, TN: Sea Raven Press, 2013

———. *The Quotable Alexander H. Stephens: Selections From the Writings and Speeches of the Confederacy's First Vice President.* Spring Hill, TN: Sea Raven Press, 2013 Sesquicentennial Civil War Edition.

———. *Give This Book to a Yankee! A Southern Guide to the Civil War for Northerners.* Spring Hill, TN: Sea Raven Press, 2014.

———. *The Articles of Confederation Explained: A Clause-by-Clause Study of America's First Constitution.* Spring Hill, TN: Sea Raven Press, 2014.

———. *Confederate Blood and Treasure: An Interview With Lochlainn Seabrook.* Spring Hill, TN: Sea Raven Press, 2015.

———. *Nathan Bedford Forrest and the Battle of Fort Pillow: Yankee Myth, Confederate Fact.* Spring Hill, TN: Sea Raven Press, 2015.

———. *Everything You Were Taught About American Slavery War is Wrong, Ask a Southerner!* Spring Hill, TN: Sea Raven Press, 2015.

———. *Confederacy 101: Amazing Facts You Never Knew About America's Oldest Political Tradition.* Spring Hill, TN: Sea Raven Press, 2015.

———. *The Great Yankee Coverup: What the North Doesn't Want You to Know About Lincoln's War!* Spring Hill, TN: Sea Raven Press, 2015.

———. *Slavery 101: Amazing Facts You Never Knew About America's "Peculiar Institution."* Spring Hill, TN: Sea Raven Press, 2015.

———. *Confederate Flag Facts: What Every American Should Know About Dixie's Southern Cross.* Spring Hill, TN: Sea Raven Press, 2016.

——. *Nathan Bedford Forrest and the Ku Klux Klan: Yankee Myth, Confederate Fact*. Spring Hill, TN: Sea Raven Press, 2016.

——. *Seabrook's Bible Dictionary of Traditional and Mystical Christian Doctrines*. Spring Hill, TN: Sea Raven Press, 2016.

——. *Everything You Were Taught About African-Americans and the Civil War is Wrong, Ask a Southerner!* Spring Hill, TN: Sea Raven Press, 2016.

——. *Nathan Bedford Forrest and African-Americans: Yankee Myth, Confederate Fact*. Spring Hill, TN: Sea Raven Press, 2016.

——. *Women in Gray: A Tribute to the Ladies Who Supported the Southern Confederacy*. Spring Hill, TN: Sea Raven Press, 2016.

——. *Lincoln's War: The Real Cause, the Real Winner, the Real Loser*. Spring Hill, TN: Sea Raven Press, 2016.

——. *The Unholy Crusade: Lincoln's Legacy of Destruction in the American South*. Spring Hill, TN: Sea Raven Press, 2017.

——. *Abraham Lincoln Was a Liberal, Jefferson Davis Was a Conservative: The Missing Key to Understanding the American Civil War*. Spring Hill, TN: Sea Raven Press, 2017.

——. *All We Ask is to be Let Alone: The Southern Secession Fact Book*. Spring Hill, TN: Sea Raven Press, 2017.

——. *The Ultimate Civil War Quiz Book: How Much Do You Really Know About America's Most Misunderstood Conflict?* Spring Hill, TN: Sea Raven Press, 2017.

——. *Rise Up and Call Them Blessed: Victorian Tributes to the Confederate Soldier, 1861-1901*. Spring Hill, TN: Sea Raven Press, 2017.

——. *Victorian Confederate Poetry: The Southern Cause in Verse, 1861-1901*. Spring Hill, TN: Sea Raven Press, 2018.

——. *Confederate Monuments: Why Every American Should Honor Confederate Soldiers and Their Memorials*. Spring Hill, TN: Sea Raven Press, 2018.

——. *The God of War: Nathan Bedford Forrest as He Was Seen by His Contemporaries*. Spring Hill, TN: Sea Raven Press, 2018.

——. *The Battle of Spring Hill: Recollections of Confederate and Union Soldiers*. Spring Hill, TN: Sea Raven Press, 2018.

——. *I Rode With Forrest! Confederate Soldiers Who Served With the World's Greatest Cavalry Leader*. Spring Hill, TN: Sea Raven Press, 2018.

——. *The Battle of Nashville: Recollections of Confederate and Union Soldiers*. Spring Hill, TN: Sea Raven Press, 2018.

Snyder, Ann E. *The Civil War From a Southern Stand-point*. Nashville, TN: self-published, 1890.

Steel, Samuel Augustus. *The South Was Right*. Columbia, SC: R. L. Bryan Co., 1914.

Stephens, Alexander Hamilton. *Speech of Mr. Stephens, of Georgia, on the War and Taxation*. Washington, D.C.: J & G. Gideon, 1848.

——. *A Constitutional View of the Late War Between the States; Its Causes, Character, Conduct and Results*. 2 vols. Philadelphia, PA: National Publishing, Co., 1870.

——. *Recollections of Alexander H. Stephens: His Diary Kept When a Prisoner at Fort Warren, Boston Harbour, 1865*. New York, NY: Doubleday, Page, and Co., 1910.

Thompson, Holland. *The New South: A Chronicle of Social and Industrial Evolution*. New Haven, CT: Yale University Press, 1920.

Van Horne, Thomas B. *History of the Army of the Cumberland: Its Organization, Campaigns, and Battles*. 2 vols. Cincinnati, OH: Robert Clarke and Co., 1875.

Warner, Ezra J. *Generals in Gray: Lives of the Confederate Commanders*. 1959. Baton Rouge, LA: Louisiana State University Press, 1989 ed.

——. *Generals in Blue: Lives of the Union Commanders*. 1964. Baton Rouge, LA: Louisiana State University Press, 2006 ed.

Watkins, Samuel Rush. *"Co. Aytch," Maury Grays, First Tennessee Regiment; or A Side Show of the Big Show*. 1882. Chattanooga, TN: self-published, 1900 ed.

Wilson, John Laird. *The Pictorial History of the Great Civil War: Its Causes, Origin, Conduct and Results*. Philadelphia, PA: The National Publishing Co., 1878.

Woods, Thomas E., Jr. *The Politically Incorrect Guide to American History*. Washington, D.C.: Regnery, 2004.

Wooldrige, John (ed.). *History of Nashville, Tenn*. Nashville, TN: H. W. Crew, 1890.

MEET THE AUTHOR

LOCHLAINN SEABROOK, a neo-Victorian and world acclaimed man of letters, is a Kentucky Colonel and the winner of the prestigious Jefferson Davis Historical Gold Medal for his "masterpiece," *A Rebel Born: A Defense of Nathan Bedford Forrest*. A classic littérateur and an unreconstructed Southern historian, he is an award-winning author, "Civil War" scholar, Confederate culture expert, Bible authority, the leading popularizer of American Civil War history, and a traditional Southern Agrarian of Scottish, English, Irish, Dutch, Welsh, German, and Italian extraction.

A child prodigy of Revolutionary, Southern, and Confederate blood, Seabrook is today a true Renaissance Man whose occupational titles also include encyclopedist, lexicographer, musician, artist, graphic designer, genealogist, photographer, and award-winning poet. Also a songwriter and a screenwriter, he has a 40 year background in historical nonfiction writing and is a member of the Sons of Confederate Veterans, the Civil War Trust, and the National Grange.

Known to his many fans as the "voice of the traditional South," due to similarities in their writing styles, ideas, and literary works, Seabrook is also often referred to as the "new Shelby Foote," the "Southern Joseph Campbell," and the "American Robert Graves" (his English cousin). Seabrook coined the terms "South-shaming" and "Lincolnian liberalism," and holds the world's record for writing the most books on Nathan Bedford Forrest. In addition, Seabrook is the first Civil War scholar to connect the early American nickname for the U.S., "The Confederate States of America," with the Southern Confederacy that arose eight decades later, and the first to note that in 1860 the party platforms of the two major political parties were the opposite of what they are today (Victorian Democrats were Conservatives, Victorian Republicans were Liberals).

Above, Colonel Lochlainn Seabrook, "the voice of the traditional South," award-winning Civil War scholar and unreconstructed Southern historian. America's most popular and prolific pro-South author, his many books have introduced hundreds of thousands to the truth about the War for Southern Independence. He coined the phrase "South-shaming" and holds the world record for writing the most books on Nathan Bedford Forrest.

The son of a Kentucky trainman and the grandson of Appalachian coal-mining and farming families, Seabrook is a seventh-generation Kentuckian whose European ancestors came from Virginia, North Carolina, and Tennessee, settling in the Bluegrass State in the early 1700s, thereafter spreading into West Virginia, the Midwest, and finally the West. He has over a dozen ancestors who fought in the American Revolutionary War, including such family surnames as Bentley, Combs, Mullins, Crase/Kress, Adkins, Kelly, Nelson, Shannon, McBrayer, Hutchinson, and Leslie.

Seabrook is co-chair of the Jent/Gent Family Committee (Kentucky), founder and director of the Blakeney Family Tree Project, and a board member of the Friends of Colonel Benjamin E. Caudill. His literary works have been endorsed by leading authorities, museum curators, award-winning historians, bestselling authors, celebrities, filmmakers, noted scientists, well regarded educators, TV show hosts and producers, renowned military artists, esteemed Southern organizations, and distinguished academicians from around the world.

Seabrook has authored over 60 popular adult books on the American Civil War, American and international slavery, the U.S. Confederacy (1781), the Southern Confederacy (1861), religion, theology, thealogy, Jesus, the Bible, the Apocrypha, the Law of Attraction, alternative health, spirituality, ghost stories, the paranormal, ufology, social issues, and cross-cultural studies of the family and marriage. His Confederate biographies, pro-South studies, Victorian Southern literature titles, genealogical monographs, family histories, biographical and military encyclopedias, self-help guides, and etymological dictionaries have received wide acclaim.

Seabrook's eight children's books include a Southern guide to the "Civil War," a biography of Nathan Bedford Forrest, a dictionary of religion and myth, a rewriting of the King Arthur legend (which reinstates the original pre-Christian motifs), two bedtime stories for preschoolers, a naturalist's guidebook to owls, a worldwide look at the family, and an examination of the Near-Death Experience.

Of blue-blooded Southern stock through his Kentucky, Tennessee, Virginia, North Carolina and West Virginia ancestors, he is a direct descendant of European royalty via his 6th great-grandfather, the Earl of Oxford, after which London's famous Harley Street is named. Among his celebrated male Celtic ancestors is Robert the Bruce, King of Scotland, Seabrook's 22nd great-grandfather. The 21st great-grandson of Edward I "Longshanks" Plantagenet), King of England, Seabrook is a 17th-generation Southerner through his descent from the colonists of Jamestown, Virginia (1607).

The 2nd, 3rd, and 4th great-grandson of dozens of Confederate soldiers, one of his closest connections to Lincoln's War is through his 3rd great-grandfather, Elias Jent Sr., who fought for the Confederacy in the Thirteenth Cavalry Kentucky under Seabrook's 2nd cousin, Colonel Benjamin E. Caudill. The Thirteenth,

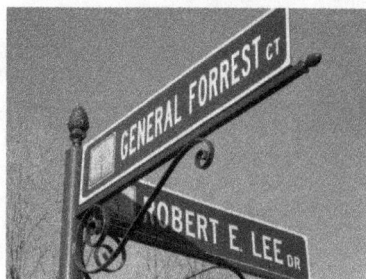

(Photo © Lochlainn Seabrook)

also known as "Caudill's Army," fought in numerous conflicts, including the Battles of Saltville, Gladsville, Mill Cliff, Poor Fork, Whitesburg, and Leatherwood.

Seabrook is a direct descendant of the families of Alexander H. Stephens, John Singleton Mosby, William Giles Harding, and Edmund Winchester Rucker, and is related to the following Confederates and other 18th- and 19th-Century luminaries: Robert E. Lee, Stephen Dill Lee, Stonewall Jackson, Nathan Bedford Forrest, James Longstreet, John Hunt Morgan, Jeb Stuart, Pierre G. T. Beauregard (approved the Confederate Battle Flag design), George W. Gordon, John Bell Hood, Alexander Peter Stewart, Arthur M. Manigault, Joseph Manigault, Charles Scott Venable, Thornton A. Washington, John A. Washington, Abraham Buford, Edmund W. Pettus, Theodrick "Tod" Carter, John B. Womack, John H. Winder, Gideon J. Pillow, States Rights Gist, Henry R. Jackson, John Lawton Seabrook, John C. Breckinridge, Leonidas Polk, Zachary Taylor, Sarah Knox Taylor (first wife of Jefferson Davis), Richard Taylor, Davy Crockett, Daniel Boone, Meriwether Lewis (of the Lewis and Clark Expedition) Andrew Jackson, James K. Polk, Abram Poindexter Maury (founder of Franklin, TN), Zebulon Baird Vance, Thomas

Jefferson, Edmund Jennings Randolph, George Wythe Randolph (grandson of Jefferson), Felix K. Zollicoffer, Fitzhugh Lee, Nathaniel F. Cheairs, Jesse James, Frank James, Robert Brank Vance, Charles Sidney Winder, John W. McGavock, Caroline E. (Winder) McGavock, David Harding McGavock, Lysander McGavock, James Randal McGavock, Randal William McGavock, Francis McGavock, Emily McGavock, William Henry F. Lee, Lucius E. Polk, Minor Meriwether (husband of noted pro-South author Elizabeth Avery Meriwether), Ellen Bourne Tynes (wife of Forrest's chief of artillery, Captain John W. Morton), South Carolina Senators Preston Smith Brooks and Andrew Pickens Butler, and famed South Carolina diarist Mary Chesnut.

Seabrook's modern day cousins include: Patrick J. Buchanan (conservative author), Cindy Crawford (model), Shelby Lee Adams (Letcher Co., Kentucky, photographer), Bertram Thomas Combs (Kentucky's 50th governor), Edith Bolling (second wife of President Woodrow Wilson), and actors Andy Griffith, Riley Keough, George C. Scott, Robert Duvall, Reese Witherspoon, Lee Marvin, Rebecca Gayheart, and Tom Cruise.

Seabrook's screenplay, *A Rebel Born*, based on his book of the same name, has been signed with acclaimed filmmaker Christopher Forbes (of Forbes Film). Set for release as a full-length feature film, it is in pre-production, awaiting the necessary funding. This will be the first movie ever made of Nathan Bedford Forrest's life story, and as a historically accurate project written from the Southern perspective, is destined to be one of the most talked about Civil War films of all time.

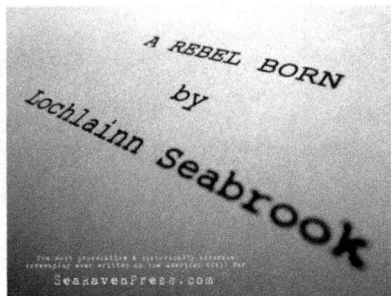

Born with music in his blood, Seabrook is an award-winning, multi-genre, BMI-Nashville songwriter and lyricist who has composed some 3,000 songs (250 albums), and whose original music has been heard in film (*A Rebel Born*, *Cowgirls 'n Angels*, *Confederate Cavalry*, *Billy the Kid: Showdown in Lincoln County*, *Vengeance Without Mercy*, *Last Step*, *County Line*, *The Mark*) and on TV and radio worldwide. A musician, producer, multi-instrumentalist, and renown performer—whose keyboard work has been variously compared to pianists from Hargus Robbins and Vince Guaraldi to Elton John and Leonard Bernstein—Seabrook has opened for groups such as the Earl Scruggs Review, Ted Nugent, and Bob Seger, and has performed privately for such public figures as President Ronald Reagan, Burt Reynolds, Loni Anderson, and Senator Edward W. Brooke. Seabrook's cousins in the music business include: Johnny Cash, Elvis Presley, Lisa Marie Presley, Billy Ray and Miley Cyrus, Patty Loveless, Tim McGraw, Lee Ann Womack, Dolly Parton, Pat Boone, Naomi, Wynonna, and Ashley Judd, Ricky Skaggs, the Sunshine Sisters, Martha Carson, and Chet Atkins.

Seabrook lives with his wife and family in historic Middle Tennessee, the heart of Forrest country and the Confederacy, where his conservative Southern ancestors fought valiantly against Liberal Lincoln and the progressive North in defense of Jeffersonianism, constitutional government, and personal liberty.

For more info visit

LochlainnSeabrook.com

If you enjoyed this book you will be interested in Colonel Seabrook's other popular related titles:

☞ ABRAHAM LINCOLN WAS A LIBERAL, JEFFERSON DAVIS WAS A CONSERVATIVE
☞ EVERYTHING YOU WERE TAUGHT ABOUT THE CIVIL WAR IS WRONG, ASK A SOUTHERNER!
☞ ALL WE ASK IS TO BE LET ALONE: THE SOUTHERN SECESSION FACT BOOK
☞ EVERYTHING YOU WERE TAUGHT ABOUT AMERICAN SLAVERY IS WRONG, ASK A SOUTHERNER!
☞ CONFEDERATE FLAG FACTS: WHAT EVERY AMERICAN SHOULD KNOW ABOUT DIXIE'S SOUTHERN CROSS
☞ LINCOLN'S WAR: THE REAL CAUSE, THE REAL WINNER, THE REAL LOSER

Available from Sea Raven Press and wherever fine books are sold

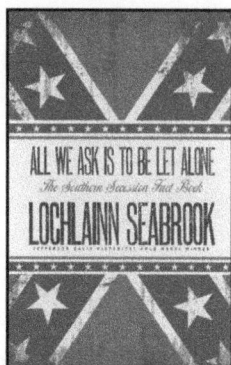

ALL OF OUR BOOK COVERS ARE AVAILABLE AS 11" X 17" POSTERS, SUITABLE FOR FRAMING

SeaRavenPress.com • NathanBedfordForrestBooks.com